Lovecasts

His *Star Sign Secrets* Revealed!

Lovecasts

The Astrological Guide to Finding *Lasting* Love

JUDI VITALE
Astrology Researcher for *Marie Claire*

Aadamsmedia
Avon, Massachusetts

Published by
Adams Media, a division of F+W Media, Inc.
57 Littlefield Street, Avon, MA 02322. U.S.A.
www.adamsmedia.com

A Hollan Publishing, Inc.
concept

ISBN 10: 1-4405-1101-2
ISBN 13: 978-1-4405-1101-1
eISBN 10: 1-4405-1139-X
eISBN 13: 978-1-4405-1139-4

Printed in the United States of America.

10 9 8 7 6 5 4 3 2 1

Library of Congress Cataloging-in-Publication Data
Vitale, Judi.
Lovecasts / Judi Vitale.
p. cm.
ISBN 978-1-4405-1101-1
1. Astrology. 2. Love—Miscellanea. I. Title.
BF1729.L6V57 2011
133.5'864677—dc22
2010038811

DEDICATION

This book is dedicated to all who wish to work on their relationships, as well as those who helped fulfill my dream of making this book come to life. My parents provided everything I needed to follow my passions and more; and my son has given me a reason to work hard so I could provide for him. My friends have encouraged me and held me up, and been a source of inspiration and love. My teachers, Joanna Shannon and Virginia Monaghan in particular, encouraged me and unselfishly shared their wisdom about astrology and writing, respectively. After many years of my own hard work putting it all together, my agent, Holly Schmidt, gave birth to this idea and opened the world of authorship to me. May all of them, and everyone who reads this book, share in the incomparable joy of lasting love.

TABLE OF CONTENTS

INTRODUCTION

Finding love is one thing, but keeping it can be far more complicated! Fortunately, you have astrology and this book to help you find your path to lasting happiness.

The zodiac sign the Sun occupied when a person is born can tell you much about an individual's personality and the way he will approach relationships. Rather than making you track down his profile and yours and spend hours trying to understand how they could possibly fit together, *Lovecasts* makes your astrological research easy. All you have to know are the month and date of your birth and the birthday of the guy you can't get enough of. And if there's no one in your life right now, you can read about each Sun Sign to see how you'll get along with guys of every kind, so you will recognize and impress Mr. Right when he comes along.

Many astrology books like to stress the concept of "good" and "bad" sign combinations, but *Lovecasts* is different. Astrology is a very complex art and science, and the understanding that your Sun Signs don't "match" doesn't take away the fact you love being together. Other factors and unique astrology patterns can compel you to like a person and allow feelings of attraction to grow into love. Because they represent your most basic natures, your signs will present opportunities and challenges that you'll work with to build a future together. The key is to understand what those are and how to make them mesh in ways that lead to happiness—and *Lovecasts* will help you achieve this kind of harmony!

Each chapter in this book is about a sign and how it shapes the way guys behave. You'll find tips on how to get a guy, what to do once you're involved with a guy, and how to keep your love growing over the long haul. You'll also get some interesting tidbits about how each sign handles various aspects of life plus scorecards on sign-to-sign compatibility.

It's important to note that, despite the scores, *every match is possible*. The scores simply reflect more how much work it's going to take for you to find that equilibrium where the two of you know your boundaries and are comfortable and happy being together. While no one can predict exactly what will happen in your relationship, this book should be read in the spirit of getting to know yourself and others so you can take some very basic traits and use them to build meaningful and joyful relationships.

As you read, keep in mind that everyone has something to offer. Coming to accept both your strengths and your partner's—and how they clash and blend with another—will help you fulfill the main purpose of being with another person: to learn and to grow. So, open your heart and read on to find your way to lasting love!

A Note about "On the Cusp"

In my view, there really isn't such a thing as a person being "on the cusp," or sharing the characteristics of two Sun Signs. When you were born, the Sun was in one zodiac sign or another. If you're looking up a birthday within a few days of two signs, you can either go online to calculate the full birth chart and find out exactly which sign ruled on that day and year or get a professional astrologer to do it for you. Some people can tell from the descriptions of the signs which one they identify with most. Whether your get it calculated or instinctively know which one is yours, once you pick a Sun Sign, stick to it!

CHAPTER 1

Aries (March 21–April 20)

YOUR MISSION: Let Him Think You're His Conquest

Aries's Potential Pluses

- Enthusiastic
- Honest
- Forceful
- Protective
- Incisive
- Smart
- Passionate
- Willing to learn
- Demonstrative
- Inspiring

Aries's Potential Minuses

- Impulsive
- Impetuous
- Brutish
- Possessive
- Unfeeling
- Ruthless
- Ignorant
- Brash
- Insulting
- Insensitive

WHAT THE ARIES GUY HAS TO GIVE . . .

The spontaneous, energetic Aries Guy is always looking for excitement. There's a good reason why his sign's symbol is the irascible-yet-impish ram: he makes the rules and is always first in line, no matter how many people he has to push aside. The intensely energetic planet Mars rules his strong and valiant personality, making action, assertiveness, and audacity his trademarks.

The Aries Guy dives head first into everything he does before he thinks about the consequences. His impulsiveness makes it easy to tell when he's happy and impossible to miss when he's mad. While he can be a successful partner and protective advocate, his childlike qualities can cause him to be impatient and inconsistent. Aries needs your love to regulate his considerable personal power and channel it toward useful activities.

As a Date:

The Aries Guy is very much a "What You See Is What You Get" kind of person. He can't help but show you who he is—a proud, strong, and fearless man who's out to make you his conquest. He won't ask if you're into him: he'll assume it! The Aries Guy always figures everyone is looking at him, so he'll assume you noticed him even before he saw you standing there! Acting like this was the case will only earn you points with him. Let him drag you back to his den, and he'll be yours forever.

Though your flexibility may snare his interest, any indecisiveness will turn Aries off in an instant—and neither of you wants that to happen. If you don't say what you want right away, he'll make a choice on your behalf. Warn him if you have strong preferences: you could get raw meat and three-alarm hot sauce when you wanted a salad!

And if you think his decision-making is quick, wait till he calls long before he said he would. This guy hates to wait for anything, especially another chance to be with you!

He will likely take you on dates to places that are heavy on action, from ball games to loud, wild clubs. If he takes you to a movie, count on adventure or comedy rather than drama. To Aries, blood and gore are fuel for his inner fire. But don't get scared! This lust for toughness will manifest as his desire to take you under his protection, in the spirit of justice and conquest. In bed, of course, this will only make him more appealing.

As a Sex Partner:

Aries will probably move in on you much faster than you expect. He's a very assertive lover and will start off by taking the "top" position. He can be tamed over time, usually through rewards. He loves to have his head rubbed, and his forehead is an especially sensual point. Press hard here—that skull can be rather thick!

Just because he doesn't ask what you want right away, don't think he doesn't care. He simply can't wait to be with you—naked and alone—and while you've been thinking about whether the timing is right, he's been planning out exactly when and how he'll ravish you.

His orgasms are extremely intense, but they can come disappointingly quickly. The best way to avoid this problem is to prolong your Aries Guy's titillation through teasing him. At first this will drive him nuts, but once he sees the benefits to waiting, it'll drive him crazy—in a good way!

As a Domestic Partner:

The Aries Guy should probably live in a cave, and unless you want your home to resemble a primitive dwelling, be prepared to clean up after him. He'll be great at hauling garbage and piling up boxes, but less adept at delicate tasks such as day-to-day repairs. Cooking will appeal to him, though—especially grilling!

This hyperactive man will rely on you to provide a quiet setting where he can actually slow down some. He'll appreciate knowing you put extra thought into preparing his favorite foods and downloading the movies he adores, just so you can share in his excitement. Loud music and bright colors, in some odd way, relax his spirit and turn him into a gentle lamb.

Emotionally:

The Aries Guy shows emotions, both good and bad, whether you want to know what he's feeling or not. In fact, he has a hard time containing them. This is "man's man" in that he doesn't mince words or waste time playing games. He wants you to look up to him and consider him to be your protector.

He rarely gets depressed and is an optimistic, "glass half full" kind of guy. But when he gets mad, stay back! His volcanic temper can seem to come out of nowhere. The good news is he'll tell you why he's so angry, and then forget all about it. These outbursts are not easy for the faint of heart to endure, and his apologies don't flow freely either. "Forgive and forget" is his motto, and if you want to get along, it would be smart to make it yours as well.

FIND YOUR ARIES GUY!

Aries's self-assurance may make kindling a romance with him simple, but that won't always be the case. There's more to making the Aries Guy feel like he's the one who's winning you over than playing to his ego: the minute he feels "caught," he'll run right back into the woods.

Being on time is a big deal to Aries, too, and he'll be just early enough to annoy you. Pretend you think it's another of his quirks, just like the grunting and having the shortest attention span you've ever seen.

Find your sign in this section to learn how your stars will help you find—and attract—the Aries Guy you've been eyeing! Then, once you've allowed him to make you "his," use your new love, passion, and a little patience to keep the fire going.

Aries

When you and your fellow Aries first get into the same room, you might want to make sure it has rubber walls! The outflow of energy from each of you will be extremely intense, but in an almost eerie way, you can complement one another and calm each other down.

He'll love not having to explain himself or make excuses for his impulsive acts, and you'll adore having a man who doesn't judge your own need to do and see everything first. Take turns choosing where you'll go for a date: you both have great ideas, and although they'll be compatible, they won't always be exactly the same. It's important that both of you get to assert your will.

Your temper tantrums could become dangerous, especially if they take place at the same time. Learn to take deep breaths before reacting, and maybe he'll take a cue from you and do the same. When your intense energy combines, it can ultimately produce gentle tenderness you'll both learn to appreciate.

Taurus

The Aries Guy will intrigue you, but you'll have to make a lot of changes just to keep up with him. This man is in constant motion, and in this you are his opposite! If you can compromise and make him believe he's converted you to some degree, you'll definitely turn him on.

Your steady ways will intrigue him, even if he's unable and unwilling to always slow down to your pace. He'll also like the way you seem to know how to acquire enough material comfort to please both of you, and he'll respect your protective nature. He will need you to praise him for his courage, and that won't be hard, unless you see some of his bold deeds as being downright foolish!

The Aries Guy won't stop chasing you, so you might as well give in and let him love you. Being the enthusiastic imp he is, he'll go to great lengths to make sure you enjoy sharing in his excitement. You won't be starved for attention or action as long as you stick with this man, but you might be left wondering if you'll ever get enough sleep again!

Gemini

You and the Aries Guy will be fast friends—literally! While he runs around in a physical sense, you do it mentally. You both have short attention spans, so being with someone else who's always looking for variety could be a great thing!

He'll admire your sharp mind and get off on your sense of humor. You'll both enjoy action movies, but you could feel sometimes as though you've lost him intellectually. It isn't that he's not smart: he just doesn't have to prove it. He loses interest when things get too complicated because he likes to boil them down to their essence. In this way, you're different as night and day, so be aware of the need to bridge the communication gap.

You might not love the way the Aries Guy seems to take ownership of you just by virtue of taking you out on a date. He's territorial, primitive, and—in some awkward-yet-endearing way—old-fashioned. Can he handle a girl who takes pride in her independence? If you manage this right, he'll be impressed by your strength and thrilled to know he has won you.

Cancer

You and the Aries Guy might not seem to be the perfect match, but your different halves make a whole. While he's out in the world hunting and gathering, you will nest and provide the perfect place for him to return. He'll extol your homemaking and culinary skills, and will gladly play the role of "baby" for you when you want someone to coddle.

He'll love the way you seem to know what he wants before he asks and will appreciate the fact you know what you want. You'll have to speak up if you want him to be more gentle, though. If you don't, he'll run roughshod over your emotions with no clue that he's hurt your feelings.

You *can* be a bit overly sensitive, so toughen up. Once he sees you're making some changes, he'll meet you halfway. If you become whiny, needy, or nagging, he'll run away as fast as he can. Show him you admire his bravery and trust that he'll always come home to you—and he will.

Leo

You and the Aries Guy will be very fast friends because you're equally enthusiastic, smart, and bold in word and deed. You're okay to be yourself with him because he's strong and confident enough to be proud of—rather than intimidated by—you.

He intrigues you on an intellectual level as well. He may not be a brainiac, but his thoughts are original, and he isn't afraid to talk about them. He takes a very fatherly posture toward you and will teach you new skills like sports, hunting, and one of his favorite hobbies—grilling!

You may have trouble keeping your Aries Guy on topic or task. His overly active body and mind will often lead to a short attention span. While he'll marvel at your follow-through, he won't follow your example without a whole lot of work. The good news: he'll never allow you to get in a rut. Work *with* him as much as you work *on* him and there's no limit to your happiness!

Virgo

Sparks of attraction will fly when you and the Aries Guy first meet, but you will have to work really hard to see eye-to-eye. His extreme "big picture" worldview clashes with your obsession with details. If you work together, you'll reach a happy balance.

Get his attention by pretending not to notice him. He'll wonder why you're not marveling at his appearance or listening with rapt attention to his stories from across the room. Once you start to converse, resist the urge to comment on his disheveled exterior (the outdoorsy smudges on his face, included): he'll run away if he believes you're being overly critical of his appearance.

To keep the conversation going, let him believe he has won you over with his strength, bravado, and primitive charm. Prove you can get your hands dirty, even if it means you have to eat wings without wet wipes or hand sanitizer. He has lots to teach you, as well as plenty to learn!

Libra

The Aries Guy is everything you want in a man and more. His strong and authoritative manner will turn you on, and he'll appreciate your delicate beauty. You may be opposites, but you'll be magnetically attracted to each other!

While gentle Venus rules your sign, aggressive Mars rules his. This is the ideal mixture for a healthy relationship, and you'll find it easy to strike a very happy balance. You'll probably assume traditional roles, and if you want him to whisk you away and sweep you off your feet, you'll have to defer to his desire to have you in his arms!

He'll love the way you seem to bring peace to even the most hostile situation, and he'll value your advice on human relationships. His temper flares can be disturbing, but if you communicate to him how disturbances of the peace can deeply hurt you, he'll try his best to change.

When two people want to please one another all the time—the way you two will—love is sure to flourish!

Scorpio

You might need to call on your reserves of patience to deal with the Aries Guy, but being with him can definitely be worth your trouble. He has qualities that impress you, and he can even keep up with you in bed!

He views you as his sex goddess, while you see him as a man who can provide you with service and support. Mars rules you both, but not in the same way. While he is the epitome of the brazen warrior, you embody the more lethal power of the stealthy Ninja. Subtlety will not be his strong suit, but as long as you realize that from the start, he won't disappoint you.

While it won't always be easy to see why you can't resist one another, your match with the Aries Guy will always be an adventure and a thrill. Spending time apart might be a good way for each of you to get the sense of autonomy you need. Then when you are together again, there will be plenty of new experiences for you to share.

Sagittarius

Electricity will flow between you and the Aries Guy from the moment you meet. His strong personality and courageous manner will attract you, while he finds your curiosity and intelligence to be a big draw.

Behind your big smiles and positive outlooks, there are big differences between you. While Aries is a "me first" kind of person, you want to serve humanity. You can combine your strengths and become an almost unstoppable force, but you'll have to learn to communicate and trust each other first. One of the hardest things about dealing with Aries is getting him to take his time.

If you want him to get even closer, show that you're willing to let him take the lead. Although neither of you will be excited to don the yoke of commitment, you'll do it with one another more easily than with anyone else. This is because you trust Aries to give you the space you need, and he knows you'll always support his desire to try something new and exciting. Together, you can't avoid finding tons of fun.

Capricorn

The Aries Guy will appeal to you because of his fiery spirit. Marvel at the way he's almost constantly in motion and challenge yourself to find ways of harnessing his energy. The first thought you have is likely to involve going to bed, but let him think that's his idea.

If you want to snag an Aries Guy, your hardest task will be letting him think he's the boss. In fact, the struggle for supremacy could be a thread that runs all through your relationship. Make it a game and you can disarm this situation to prevent it from becoming a conflict.

When you do go to bed with him, he'll know he has the sweetest and sexiest girl in town. He'll show his appreciation even more when you allow him to take the reins, even if it's only for a little while! Although he may not be a strategic match for you, when it comes to pure, pioneering energy, you might have to practice to try and keep up with him.

Aquarius

The Aries Guy's pure innocence and pronounced manliness will intrigue you. You see him as a challenge because you want to teach him about equality and respect between the sexes. Meanwhile, he may coax you into letting go of your control to simply enjoy the moment.

If you want him to whisk you away, you'll have to let him believe he's won you. This may not be easy, but it's necessary. Once you get him, you can try to work on him, but good luck! Until you learn to let him be who he is, he'll never make the kind of commitment it takes to fulfill your needs.

Your best bet is to appreciate the Aries Guy as a friend first. Because he's always jumping the gun, you'll have to play a delicate game of tug of war to keep him from going too far, too soon. There's a lot to be said for keeping him "on the chase." He'll enjoy pursuing you almost as much as he digs getting you for his own. Meanwhile, you'll be delighted to have all his high-powered attention focused on you!

Pisces

The Aries Guy can be a bit too brash for you, but that doesn't make him any less intriguing. His pure honesty will make you trust him immediately. His impish behavior will also be a constant source of amusement, as you also have a charming and endearing child's view of the world.

You can get his attention by letting him know you want him to carry you away. One of your soulful looks, coupled with a nod of the head and a sideways glance should be enough of a hint. The Aries Guy is perceptive, but it's going to be hard for him to become as sensitive and gentle as you would like. You just have to give him a fair shot.

You can be very happy together as long as you remember to have fun and keep your senses of humor. You'll love the way your relationship works because just as you're drifting off into space, he'll find a dozen reasons why you should come back down to earth to enjoy a fresh adventure with the lovable, courageous, and downright *fun* Aries Guy.

KEEP YOUR ARIES GUY!

Once your Aries Guy's short attention span expires, how do you keep the fire burning? You'll have to move at least as fast—or faster—than he does! He will continue to lead the way most of the time, but your life together will also include moments when you have to cater to him much like you would a baby. If his impatience and impulsivity get to you, remind him gently. He won't like harsh reprimands that reveal anything but your love and admiration.

Home, family, and hearth are all pretty high on your Aries Guy's list of priorities. After his long of days hunting and gathering, he'll need a spot to call his own—a "den" of sorts, where he can put the various trophies of his exploits on display. You'll be welcome to visit, if you don't mind stepping over the rugged terrain he's sure to create! He'll probably be fond of telling stories of his glory days, so prepare to smile and nod lovingly—even after the thousandth rendition!

Look for your sign in this section to learn how using the traits of your Sun Sign to understand, please, and continue to attract your Aries Guy will keep your romance going for a long time to come.

Aries

You are sure to live busy lives, both separately and as a couple. It'll be comforting to know your Aries Guy understands you and is every bit as busy as you are. You might need to make a pact, though, that forces you to avoid overbooking. If you're not careful, you could wind up with very little time to be together alone, and you won't want to miss out on the tender aspects of your relationship.

Sex is a great way for you to use your incredible energy for good purposes. The most trying part of your sexual dynamic will be you holding back from pursuing him. You'll be very cute together, as you rub heads and rush to the finish. As you get more used to each other, you'll settle down and enjoy a slower pace.

When people are moving as much and as fast as you two, there are going to be transgressions of non-neatness. Still, if you work together, your determination will eliminate any mess faster than a four-star professional cleaning crew. Your ability to act as a unit in all areas of life will make this an extraordinary, fulfilling relationship.

Taurus

The tug-of-war that takes place between you and your Aries Guy can work in favor of your relationship, as long as you give one another the space to be who you are. He can prevent you from rotting in the rut you can make for yourself, and you can soothe and inspire him.

Use your sex life as a place to work out these differences in creative ways. Tease him with slow, deliberate moves that titillate him as much as gratify his desires. In turn, when he takes over and begins to show you all the sensations your body can feel, you'll come to appreciate the virtues of the pure, unadulterated passion he has for you.

Acceptance sounds like a simple enough concept, but with you and your Aries Guy it may be difficult. You're very different people, and in order to be happy you'll have to accept your differences. Celebrate the fact that you can overlook them enough to spend time learning and growing from the gentle give-and-take of your relationship.

Gemini

Your Aries Guy will recognize that you do with your mind what he does with his body, so go out into the world to experience and understand as much as possible.

In the bedroom, he'll want you to stop talking and show him some action. You can be up for that, as long as he's willing to let you tell him what feels good and what doesn't. He'll accept instructions given in the spirit of "self-improvement," but he can get pretty wounded if you imply he's not pleasing you. Admit it when you enjoy the way he just takes over and has his way with you!

His outbursts of temper might upset you when they come along, but you'll soon see that they pass as quickly as they arise. You can talk about your feelings, but don't discuss your disputes to death. Focus on the fun you can have together, whether you're in the bedroom or out showing off what an active, intelligent, and down right fun couple you and your Aries Guy can be!

Cancer

You and your Aries Guy will settle into "couplehood" rather quickly because you both know what you want when you see it. He truly appreciates the things you do for him and will show his gratitude by constantly trying to please you.

Sexually, he'll want to be in charge most of the time, and that will be just fine with you! If you need him to slow down, the instructions you give him by touch will be far more meaningful than any words you can use. Guide his hands and other body parts to the areas where you want them. He's a fast learner!

You will have an easy time staying together because you fall effortlessly into roles that allow each of you to do half of the work of the relationship. Switch it up once in awhile so you get to taste his cooking and he can groove on watching you tackle an adventure. You're the kind of couple who'll always be there for each other.

Leo

Once you and your Aries Guy commit to taking your friendship further, your lives will become far more fulfilling. He adores the way you stand up for yourself and so willingly offer your talents to others. You love him for being so courageous and spontaneous.

Your bedroom is the perfect place to show your appreciation. Let your Aries Guy know you're ready by offering yourself to him, without making demands. That certain look you give him might be all he needs, because he seems to pick up your vibes before you even finish your thoughts.

Unfortunately, neither of you is likely to be able to tend to the household chores this telepathically. Sit down with a list of them and decide who is more capable and/or willing to do each one, and you'll dig in.

The rapport between the two of you is what will keep you together. When either of you loses your composure and engages in outbursts of anger, remember that no matter how mad you are, nothing could ever be worth losing your best friend.

Virgo

You and your Aries Guy will have to "chill" to remain happily together. He might be overly active, but you can be too regimented. Make better use of the time you have together by relaxing and doing things that allow you to unwind.

Work out some of your issues in the bedroom to help make the reasons for your relationship more clear. He'll often rush right through the act of lovemaking, but all that can change when you introduce him to techniques that create sensations he may have yet to experience.

You may have yet to experience living with a man as messy as an Aries. Find a spot for yours to keep his baseball bats and paintball guns where they won't clash with your clean and neat-as-a-pin idea of what "home" should look like.

Make this match a partnership: help him to organize and channel his energy in useful directions, and he'll help you see why it's a good idea to remain calm in the face of life's threats. Whether you're battling financial ruin or an infestation of ants, you'll always be glad to have your Aries Guy fighting by your side.

Libra

You and your Aries Guy won't need to work very hard to stay together, but there are a few things you need to know to keep one another happy. Remember that there are times when it's more important to be with him than it is to avoid breaking a nail. The more you show your willingness to try the things that turn him on, the better.

He'll more than reciprocate when he gets you in the bedroom. Although he's not the refined and gentle prince of your girlhood dreams, he is the kind of lover you've been waiting for. He'll make you feel like a goddess with the way he ravishes you, and although he can be coarse and abrupt when he's out in the world, he will always pause to put you on a pedestal when you're together, alone.

Your complementary yet contrasting qualities will keep you together. The sweetest part about your relationship is your mutual acceptance and admiration. After all, what would you do without this manly, voracious, and adoring man worshipping the ground on which you walk?

Scorpio

Hanging on to your Aries Guy will be fairly simple for you, as long as you learn to respect him from the outset. For all his innocence, he isn't one to take criticism unless it's helpful and supportive. Even then, you'll have to tread softly on his ego. The temper tantrum that can result from you hurting his feelings could even make someone as strong as you bristle!

The Aries Guy enjoys sex as much as you do and will appreciate the way you delve into the depths of your soul to offer him the things he desires. In turn, he'll give you the kind of seeing-to you'll find yourself daydreaming about hours later. The two of you can always remember what a great match you are when you're making love!

The rest of the relationship will be all about finding common ground. You might be surprised at your Aries Guy's ability to fall in love with mysteries, or your own taste for the tacky blood and gore in his beloved action movies. You are two sides of the same coin, and together you can build a relationship that's even more valuable than gold.

Sagittarius

Your Aries Guy seems so easy to get along with that you won't have too much trouble committing to your relationship. He'll love the way you're always willing to play, and although he'll want you to spend a lot of time with him, he'll never smother or hover.

You'll have more than your share of fun in the bedroom, to be sure! Your playful attitude and his desire to please will go a long way toward keeping both of you happy. You'll also find that the nonverbal rapport you have with your Aries Guy will enhance your relationship and help you work out your everyday issues and real life problems.

Keeping your bond will be easy because you are best friends in love. His childlike ways mirror your own, so you can always come up with fun things to do together. When it comes to protecting each other, though, you can get as serious as they come. You'll always be your Aries Guy's biggest advocate and fan because he brings so much excitement and adventure into your life.

Capricorn

Being with your Aries Guy could feel like taking on an apprentice, but don't become his surrogate parent! He'll want to show you how to look at life with eyes of innocence and enthusiasm as opposed to caution and respect. You will enrich one another's lives and multiply your powers by sharing your knowledge.

This will be especially obvious while you're having sex. You may believe you have a savage nature, but your Aries Guy will show you what primal lovemaking is really all about. Use your full repertoire of sensual pleasures, and he'll be grateful to find out there's even more to having great sex than he already thought!

Your home might not be the neatest, because your Aries Guy is not the most organized person you'll ever meet. You can give him some tips, but he's unlikely to pay more than cursory attention to keeping things tidy.

Messy or not, your home is sure to be full of love. You and your Aries Guy will find a nice balance between adventure and normalcy and share it with your friends. In most matters, he'll defer to your executive skills, but as long as you allow him to protect you, he'll always make you feel safe and secure.

Aquarius

You will enjoy being with your Aries Guy because he'll teach you the meaning of passion. Living in your head the way you do, it's easy to forget about your physical needs. Lucky for you, life with the Aries Guy is bound to change all that!

The magic the two of you create in bed could be reason enough to stick with your Aries Guy! Once you get past the primitive nature of his approach, you can appreciate his primal desire and enjoy showing him your appreciation. He'll love it when you rub his head or gently stroke the area around his eyes.

Housekeeping will be a challenge, with your proclivity for eclectic collections and his lack of concern for where he happens to pitch his clothing. As long as you can sit down and discuss what needs to be done, he'll roll up his sleeves and pour his heart into occasional cleaning sessions.

More than anything you'll learn to value his ability to bring you back to the basics. He has a way of un-complicating your life and showing you there can be better, truer ways to live—especially when you're wrapped tightly in his arms.

Pisces

Your choice to be with your Aries Guy can be a good one, even if your friends think he's just too rough for you. You know how he can teach you to be open to new experiences and less likely to retreat at the slightest sign of conflict. It's likely that the Aries Guy won you over by showing you what he can do in bed. His direct and passionate manner will open up your heart, and his childlike way of bonding will keep him close to you for a long time. While it may take time for him to realize what merging on the soul-level is about, he'll be eternally grateful to you for showing him what you instinctually know.

Around the house, you'll both be less conscious of what you do with your possessions than you should be. Make arrangements to clean together so you can have companionship and help while you tend to mundane chores.

Your mutual innocence will keep you together for a very long time. You're both open to life's latest adventures, and enjoying them as a couple will bring you abundant joy.

YOUR ARIES GUY AND . . .

Because he devotes himself so completely to those he loves, it's essential to know how other people will fit into your Aries's life with you. Read on for tips for getting your friends, family, his friends, and even your pets to love your Aries Guy the same way you do.

Your Female Friends

Your brusque and manly Aries Guy will accept your friends into your circle, but he might limit his one-to-one communication. In his mind, he sees himself as irresistible, and worries one of the ladies might get the wrong idea. He'll like it better when you're in the room with him and your pals, proudly staking your claim on him. He could get uncomfortable around knowing giggles between you and the girls.

Your Male Friends

Your Aries Guy will keep a close eye on any guy who gets too close to you. He likes to think you are his alone, and he'll become very competitive around men who take your attention from him, even if they don't have the least bit of sexual interest in you. He will always want to know he's won you as his prize.

His Female Friends

Your Aries Guy's female friends will probably be the kind of people who don't focus on the sexual differences between your Aries Guy and themselves, so they will truly be nonthreatening. He, on the other hand *does*, very much, see them as eligible females that he is far too noble to flirt with, because he wants to prove his devotion to you, so don't worry.

His Male Friends

There are some things you probably shouldn't see, and one of them is the stuff that happens when your Aries Guy is out with his pals. Disgusting displays of overeating and drinking usually will follow a day out playing sports or going hunting or fishing. If his pals go out "scoping" other women, he'll avoid meeting them in favor of sizing up his chances of maintaining his alpha-male position among his peers.

Your Family

Aries has a fairly solid attitude of respect and deference toward family, and will be very friendly toward yours. His "life of the party" personality will make a positive impression, because he'll tone it down to fit in perfectly with the tone and demeanor of your relatives. If they're stiff or stuffy, though, he'll try really hard to open them up. If he fails, he'll probably begin to dread future visits.

His Family

Family means a lot to your Aries Guy. Home is the place, no matter what it was like growing up, where he returns when he wants to go back to the comfort of being an innocent child. As the "baby" of the zodiac, Aries will always resist growing up fully. He's a little kid in a big package, always ready for the kind of fun, games, food, hugs, kisses, and love he can only get from the people who knew him from Day One.

Your Pets

Your Aries Guy will love animals that are rough and tumble enough for him to play with the most, but he's rather friendly with all pets. The ones with the most personality and strongest responses will score biggest with him. He'll love lapping up gravy with the Lab, but you'll also catch him cuddling kitty out of the corner of your eye.

His Pets

To the Aries Guy, a pet is something you take on as part of the family and is usually large with at least as many animalistic attributes as he has. It probably slobbers and sheds, too. Aries is much more a dog person than a cat lover, but his heart is big enough for just about any pet that responds to his own animal nature.

His Potential for Success

Hunting and gathering comes as second nature to your Aries Guy, so he's pretty good at providing the means for the two of you to live comfortably. He'll hope that you'll contribute, but especially if you have children, he won't expect it. He'll want to create a fun family life for his children, and expect you to make parenthood a priority.

His Role as a Father

Because he's a big kid, you'll rarely have to ask your Aries Guy to pay more attention to the games children play. He'll heartily get involved in their activities and is likely to even become the coach for their sports team. He may even push sports on children who would rather sit on the sidelines, but as long as you encourage him to stress moderation, it won't hurt to get the children up and moving.

ARIES COMPATIBILITY

Your Sign	Compatibility Level
Aries	♈♈♈♈
Taurus	♉♉
Gemini	♊♊♊
Cancer	♋♋♋♋♋
Leo	♌♌♌♌
Virgo	♍♍
Libra	♎♎♎♎♎
Scorpio	♏♏♏♏♏
Sagittarius	♐♐♐♐
Capricorn	♑♑♑
Aquarius	♒♒
Pisces	♓♓

ARIES SHORT-TERM PROSPECTS

Your Sign	Short-Term Prospects
Aries	♈♈♈♈♈
Taurus	♉♉
Gemini	♊♊♊
Cancer	♋♋♋♋♋
Leo	♌♌♌♌
Virgo	♍
Libra	♎♎♎♎
Scorpio	♏♏♏♏♏
Sagittarius	♐♐♐♐
Capricorn	♑♑♑♑
Aquarius	♒♒
Pisces	♓

ARIES LONG-TERM PROSPECTS

Your Sign	Long-Term Prospects
Aries	♈♈♈♈
Taurus	♉♉
Gemini	♊♊♊
Cancer	♋♋♋♋♋
Leo	♌♌♌♌
Virgo	♍♍
Libra	♎♎♎♎♎
Scorpio	♏♏♏♏♏
Sagittarius	♐♐♐♐
Capricorn	♑♑♑
Aquarius	♒♒
Pisces	♓♓

CHAPTER 2

Taurus (April 21–May 20)

YOUR MISSION: Make Him Feel Calm, Cozy, and Adored

Taurus's Potential Pluses	Taurus's Potential Minuses
• Reliable	• Boring
• Strong	• Stubborn
• Predictable	• Bullying
• Industrious	• Demanding
• Financially responsible	• Self-centered
• Tasteful	• Over-indulgent
• Domestically talented	• Materialistic
• Protective	• Stingy
• Warm	• Selfish
• Caring	• Argumentative

WHAT THE TAURUS GUY HAS TO GIVE . . .

The Taurus Guy seems to be a simple soul, but his apparently calm exterior conceals some surprises. His reputation for being slow and steady comes from his desire to protect the status quo. Just like his sign's symbol, the bull, as long as things stay the way they are, Taurus will feel strong and confident. He likes his life to be predictable, and he'll drive you nuts trying to fit everything you do into a concrete, supposedly foolproof plan. At the first sign of any randomness, though, your usually placid bull will panic as though the Picador landed one right in his back!

Possessions make him feel secure, and although he'll share some of his things with you, he's not the type of guy to give you the shirt off his back. He'll ask that you prove you have assets beyond your ravishing beauty and irresistible sexiness before he agrees to huge signs of fiscal commitment such as joint accounts or co-ownership of a home.

As a Date:

The Taurus Guy has a hard time hiding his cautious, predictable nature. Dinner and/or a movie will allow him to remain in his safety zone. You'll probably visit places where everybody knows him, because he tends to go to the same places all the time. He'll also have one thrifty eye on the price; a man can't maintain his resources if he doesn't curb his spending!

The worst thing you can do is play games with the Taurus Guy. His nervous interior will overwhelm him, and ultimately he will flee. Be honest and straightforward, and he'll move toward you. If his resources are threatened in any way, he'll respond with a colder, more calculating attitude than you thought possible. This relationship may never be a "free ride," but it can be a very passionate and sexy one!

As a Sex Partner:

Fortunately for you, the Taurus Guy absolutely adores sex! You'll see why he is called "the bull" by the way he seems to strut during the seduction and the sex act. He will approach you slowly but deliberately and be very proud of himself as he does it. You might want to say "Wow" now and then, just to keep him going. He likes to know you're enjoying what he does to please you.

He lasts a long time in bed, coming to orgasm as slowly and deliberately as he would assess the quality of merchandise in a luxury store. When he reaches a climax, though, the explosion will only be more intense because it's been contained for so long. He likes to be in control, but eventually his indulgent side takes over, and he explodes with complete abandon.

As a Domestic Partner:

There's a sense of entitlement about the Taurus Guy that makes him less inclined to volunteer for physical labor. He'll help out if you ask him, though. He'll have his own, slow and purposeful ways of doing things, and will excel at food preparation and cleanup.

He really wants you to take care of as much of the domestic work as possible, but he'd like it even better if you'd do it his way! You could get annoyed when he tries to tell you how to scrub or vacuum, and it would be okay for you to stop doing it and suggest he take over. He'll probably go back to what he was doing before, pretending neither of you said a word.

Emotionally:

The Taurus Guy's feelings can be hurt deeply, especially by disrespect and disloyalty. When he's angry, he might have to step away until he cools down. Don't engage him. If you wave the red flag in the

Bull's face, he can't be held responsible for the temper tantrum that could ensue.

Even if you think he's being cheap or too set in his ways, don't come out and say it. Suggest alternatives to what he's doing, and he's likely to get the hint. More than anything, the Taurus Guy wants to make a good impression on you and other people who are watching the way he treats you.

If he's offended, he'll mope. Your apology will help, but so will time. Before too long, he'll forgive you, and it'll take just a little bit longer for him to forget.

FIND YOUR TAURUS GUY!

The Taurus Guy is one of the most unassuming people you'll meet. He'll be thrilled that you're into him, but he'll try not to show it. Keep remembering that inside that slow, steady exterior is one very excited little boy! Tell him how much you admire the way he looks and what he's wearing, and you'll score points. Let him take you out first, though. Despite his desire to see you contribute to the relationship, his pride will push him to take the lead.

There are many ways to let the sensually attractive bull know you want to take him on. Check for your sign in this section to see how you can wave that red flag in a way that sends him rushing right into your arms.

Aries

Before you charge at the comparatively placid Bull, remind yourself to ease up. The Taurus Guy can be scared off easily, especially if he senses he's about to be overwhelmed by someone as powerful as you are. He'll be flattered if you show your interest in him by compliment-ing something he owns, or by looking at him with your enthusiastic (but not *too* eager!) smile. The Taurus Guy wants to know you respect him.

The thing that attracts you most to him is probably the calming effect he has on you. Give him a chance to slow down the pace a little, and he'll soothe you with his gentle touch and attentive ears.

Patience is his strongest virtue, so there's a lot for you to learn from him. He'll need you, at times, to blast him out of his rut. Boisterous behavior—as long as it's slightly muted—will inspire him to try new things, and he'll love playing with you, wherever you go.

Taurus

The Taurus Guy will sense you and he are cut from the same cloth and feel safe while he's around you. It might take awhile before one of you makes the first move, but let him go first. He'll like that.

His ability to manage his finances will impress you. You both know you're very capable of buying the best life has to offer, but he'll need to see evidence of your willingness to earn your keep.

The two of you can have a wonderful time exchanging ideas and immersing yourselves in pleasure. It's a beautiful thing to find a guy who thinks like you, but unless you can get some third party to police you, stay away from places that sell all your favorite things, especially chocolate! You're far more likely to say it's okay to overindulge than you are to offer one another some healthy discipline.

Gemini

The Taurus Guy has an odd sort of appeal to you, mainly because he's so different. He lives by his bodily senses, and you exist for the purpose of expanding your mind. Your curiosity tells you there's a lot to learn from him, and that alone can be quite an attraction factor.

Try introducing yourself with as few words as possible. The Taurus Guy doesn't like to be rushed into anything, and if you talk too much or too fast, he'll think you're trying to con him. Let him do some talking, too. No one is saying this will be easy for you—but you can do it!

Your sense of humor and your ability to walk right up to people and start talking will astound the Taurus Guy. You'll appreciate his dependability and the opportunity to learn more about being accountable for your own actions. You must prove your loyalty to Taurus, above all. Once he trusts you, then he'll begin to make his move . . . slowly.

Cancer

You might fall hard for the Taurus Guy, mainly because he offers what you want and need—security. He'll adore the way you cater to his wishes, but won't want you to depend on him. Show your ability to pull your own weight, and he'll probably shower you with love and affection.

The two of you feel very comfortable in one another's company, so getting to know him is easy. He'll like your sweet, gentle personality, and you'll adore his dignity and common sense. He can be just as intent on building a safe and secure nest as you are, but he can also be possessive and demanding, much like you.

The connection between you is strong, and the sexual electricity level is high. Yet, this relationship will take some work. Start by making sure you both have the same values about things that matter most to you, such as family, security and a healthy home life. The Taurus Guy won't change without a fight.

Leo

If you've been wondering when you'd finally meet your match, your answer could come when you encounter the Taurus Guy! His strong, steady, and proud manner will complement your own courageous and flashy personality. Where you want to put on a show, he wants to know how much money you'll get for doing it.

You'll like the idea of having an advocate around, and he'll be entertained by the way you have no fear of performing in front of a crowd. He'll notice, even from afar, that you have a certain spark, and that the two of you could make fantastic music together.

Although he'll admire your talents, he won't compete with you for attention. He'd rather stand just outside the spotlight and watch you shine, at least in public. He sees you as someone who can offer him safety and protection. Spend as much time as possible convincing him he's right.

Virgo

You'll be enamored with the Taurus Guy right away, because he's so practical, strong, and seemingly steady. Your way of making things—even work—seem like fun will really appeal to him, and you'll both enjoy basic entertainment that makes you laugh and forget your worries.

If you want to get to know him better, just strike up a friendly conversation. The Taurus Guy will want to be able to talk to you, first and foremost. Meanwhile, you'll enjoy listening to what he has to say and learning more about the world of accumulating resources than you might already know.

The two of you will have a great connection, but it could take awhile for passion to develop. The Taurus Guy moves very slowly, and you take awhile to warm up to your love partners, too. Don't mistake his distance for a lack of interest. Your respect matters a lot to him, and until he's sure he has it, he won't put it at risk.

Libra

The Taurus Guy is an enigma to you. It seems to make sense that you would get along from your first meeting, because Venus rules both of your signs. The truth is, a basic disconnect between you will make you work harder to come together. You'll need to devote a lot of time to getting to understand him, and getting him to trust you.

The Taurus Guy is very centered on his material holdings, and he's also extremely protective of them. Unlike you, he's not fond of pursuing ideas just for the intellectual exercise of it all. He likes to know there will be some practical use for all the knowledge he accumulates.

Despite all this, you find the Taurus Guy extremely sexy! You will want to jump on him from the moment you meet, but he will want you to wait until he's ready to invite you to do just that. Once you get that part down, you're likely to find your sensual connection is the core that keeps your relationship strong.

Scorpio

The sometimes stubborn, often immovable, and very charming Taurus Guy isn't for everyone, but he's absolutely perfect for you! His earthy nature is the ultimate complement to your watery, emotional soul, while your ability to see beneath the surface opens his eyes to the unseen as well as that which is right in his face.

He doesn't fear you, as many others do, and you'll like that. He'll feel oddly comfortable when he's around you, as though he's found the one person in this world who can stand up to him and fight for what she believes in, and this excites him beyond belief!

Although he won't always freely share the things he has (for fear he might lose them!), you won't mind. You have ways of accruing your own material wealth, and the love of the Taurus Guy is far more important to you than any item you might take on as a possession.

Sagittarius

Your first impression of the Taurus Guy might not be a very good one, but eventually, this practical-minded, strong, and quiet person could grow on you. You'll like the way he can enjoy himself no matter where he is, and he'll love your creativity and sense of humor.

He'll be so flattered when he finds out someone as dynamic as you is into him. Yet, you'll have to overcome differences in outlook. He's ultragrounded and practical, and often fails to see the point of you running off on some loosely defined adventure.

He may like to travel with you at some point in your relationship, but he'll definitely prefer first class! Value to the Taurus Guy comes in two forms: enjoyment and hard cash. You'll get used to his sensibilities as time goes on, but you'll have to work hard to reach a point where the two of you see eye to eye.

Capricorn

The Taurus Guy seems to fit perfectly into your idea of friendship and love. His sense of humor blends well with yours, and he adores the way you take chaotic situations and organize them so everyone involved can be productive.

Getting to know him better is easy. The moment you start to talk, the Taurus Guy will open up. He'll sense he can trust you, and he'll pick up on your very sexy vibe. Like you, he enjoys the pleasures of the flesh, and indulges in them more feverishly than most people. You might decide to go to bed much faster than most couples, but you won't regret it.

Remember that your Taurus Guy will want as much or more respect than you want from him. Go out of your way to make time to be together. Two people who are so focused on work will truly benefit from having one another's company as a way to escape the daily grind.

Aquarius

The Taurus Guy might not seem like your type, but the two of you will make excellent partners. Both of you are very sure of what you think and feel, and you won't waver under pressure. Together, you can build a life that balances idealism and practicality.

Once he knows you understand and respect him, he'll ask you questions about your interests. Taurus will appreciate that you have your own, distinct set of activities and enough independence to assure him you won't become a "leech."

There may be times when you don't agree, and this could come up when you get involved in community and political causes. Unless your Taurus Guy sees what's in it for him, his interest—and investment—will be very limited. It's best to focus on your personal lives, and the things you can do together that let you be strong individuals who aren't afraid to celebrate your similarities.

Pisces

You and the Taurus Guy will make a very sweet couple because you're both searching for safety and security. His strength and steadiness will create a safe harbor for you, while your softness and kindness will envelop him in the comfort he seeks.

When you first meet, talk about the things that you both like, such as music, good food, and fine art. Once the Taurus Guy sees your love for the finer things in life he'll be very attracted to your sensitivity. The way you seem to care for him without asking anything in return inspires his generous spirit, so he could begin your relationship by offering you some pretty nifty gifts.

As time goes on, you'll come to see that what Taurus values more than anything is the unconditional love you offer him. Walk in the rain, talk on the phone, or have a little picnic in the park. He'll love doing all those little, loving things that don't cost a penny.

KEEP YOUR TAURUS GUY!

Because the Taurus Guy is a creature of habit, you might think he would always stay in a relationship, but that's not the case. This pleasure-loving, strong-willed creature will need to have a good reason to stick it out. Pushing his "happy" buttons, including the one that creates pleasure, is a good way to start. Let him know you want to please him, and don't stop pouring on the sensual stimuli.

Getting along with the Taurus Guy is easy, but he can be a pain when you can't get him to see anything but his point of view. If you make promises, keep them. His temper flares can be wild, and you won't want to find yourself on the wrong end of them. Unconditional love is a great policy to follow. The more you practice it, the more cooperation you'll receive from your Taurus Guy.

Look in this section for a peek of what long-term love will be like with your Taurus Guy, and to discover ways to keep the fire burning in years to come.

Aries

While he has his own faults, your Taurus Guy will also point out a lot of yours—especially the ones that involve impatience and impulsiveness. You could slow down, but at the same time, you'll be wondering when he's going to speed up. In bed, Taurus is a whole lot of fun. He'll love everything you do for him, and he'll also cater to your needs.

His pace in bed could take some time to adjust to, but once you get there, you'll realize the benefits of not taking in everything all at once. Aim for his neck if you want to watch his whole body shiver with delight!

While his metered way of life helps in some areas, he's not likely to take as much time cleaning house. A frank talk about who should be doing what work might help, but he'll try to get out of the heavy lifting. You'll have to let that garbage fester until he realizes you're not going to take it out for him.

Your playful attitude—and ever-developing tolerance—will help you gain happiness with your Taurus Guy.

Taurus

It's fun to live with your fellow Taurus, but you'll both have to compensate for some of your mutual shortcomings. Because neither of you will be inclined to start new projects, one of you is going to have to become the "go-to" half of the couple. You'll also need to set up boundaries on shared finances to keep it fair.

Next to your favorite restaurant, the bedroom will be the place you love the most. You might even set up a mini-spa in the master bath that allows you to enjoy facials, mutual massages, and long soaks in the extra-large tub together. Languishing in luxury is a turn-on neither of the two of you will want to resist.

Because you're so content with what's familiar, it's hard to incorporate new elements into your home and social life. Adopt a friend or two who can drag you along to places you haven't gone before, and you'll avoid burning out on the same-ol'-same-ol'. Getting stuck in a rut will stunt your relationship's growth, and neither of you want that.

Gemini

You'll need your sense of humor to stay happy while you develop your long-term relationship with the Taurus Guy. He's so cute, yet so impossibly predictable! Coax him to try new things. Once you get him moving, he'll be glad you inspired him.

In bed, you won't have to work so hard at getting him started. The Taurus Guy embodies sensuality and will probably ask for sex more than you wish he would! Try it his way. The great thing about having lots of sex with your Taurus Guy is it leaves you with less flirting time. Disloyalty is something your Taurus Guy won't stand for, so if you can't stop yourself from flitting between the flowers, don't let him see or hear about it.

Despite your differences, you and your Taurus Guy can be very happy. You're a big talker, and he's a great listener. Work that winning combination so you can achieve communication, understanding, and true love!

Cancer

You and your Taurus Guy both enjoy the comforts of home. He takes a hand in helping you arrange things the way he likes them, and you share a family-type bond that keeps you close on all kinds of levels.

If you had the time, the two of you could easily spend most of your lives in bed. Not only do you love having sex, you're huge on cuddling and cherish lazing around in each other's arms. Eventually, you'll get up to take care of someone or something else, but your Taurus Guy might not!

While you're very focused on children, pets, and family, he's less prone to disrupt his plans for their convenience. You may have to deal with these matters more as a solo act than as part of a couple.

To remain blissfully united with your Taurus Guy, adjust your expectations to match his tendencies. Work at compromise to create the harmony and domestic tranquility that will keep both of you happy.

Leo

You and your Taurus Guy can keep a very healthy attitude about your relationship, and that's why you have such a great chance at long-term happiness. Your individual strengths will keep you from dominating one another, while they create a bond that lets you enjoy mutual respect and admiration.

The two of you worship one another in bed, and that's a great recipe for the kind of hot stuff that will keep your love burning for years. He appreciates your beauty and courage, and you adore his stability and nobility.

Around the house, it's not going to be easy to get him moving so you'll have to outsmart him. Remind him of how proud he'll be when he finishes the chores.

The two of you will be very content with one another, yet you'll encourage each other to grow stronger as individuals. Show your Taurus Guy how much you love him, and he'll be yours for as long as you'd like!

Virgo

You and your Taurus Guy share a common bond of taking practical action and conserving your resources. You also enjoy the same kinds of fun and have the discipline to balance recreation with hard work.

In bed, the two of you will have to get used to one another. While you approach sex with a matter of fact, direct attitude, he's far less cerebral about it. Your Taurus Guy is a sensual creature, whose desire is expressed without thought or word. Let him lead you to a whole new level of orgasmic pleasure.

Around the house, you'll be neater, but he'll also have high standards. He can occasionally splurge and sometimes destroy your budget, so keep an eye on his spending.

Although this might not be the all-consuming passion of steamy novels, your realistic and functional relationship has the potential for the kind of "happy ever after" factor other couples can only dream about.

Libra

You and your Taurus Guy can easily create a close relationship. The only problem is, you'll so love being together, you could happily brush aside your other responsibilities. Promise to keep one another honest, and you'll be okay.

In the bedroom, he'll worship you in the way you like to be regarded. Offer him a variety of ways to achieve pleasure and be sure to show him how impressed you are by the explosive power of his orgasms.

When it comes time to deal with household duties, let him do something because he excels at it. This will give him the incentive to dive right in there, leaving you free to make the rest of the house beautiful.

Your Taurus Guy is no dummy. Just because he adores you, don't expect him to give you everything you want. He will challenge you to pull your own weight, so show him you have the ability to take care of business at home and in the work world as well.

Scorpio

The utter contentment you'll feel while with your Taurus Guy will astound you. It might seem like a dream to have found someone who's as strong and steadfast as you are and still willing to see things your way, now and then! You'll do your best to keep the relationship going in every way because it's mutually supportive and sustaining.

In bed, your Taurus Guy meets you with a sexual intensity that allows you to open up and welcome him into your heart and soul. Your mysterious nature intrigues him. He'll love it when you wear lingerie that only shows off certain parts of your body here and there.

Around the house, you'll work things out and split the chores according to who does what best. Even if his bed-making and bathroom cleaning don't meet your standards of perfection, a sample of his cooking and coffee making will quickly redeem his domestic skills in your eyes.

The secret to your happiness is appreciating what's different about you as much as what's the same. Your deep emotional nature and his practical approach combine to sustain two individuals who become stronger and even more powerful when they join forces.

Sagittarius

You and your Taurus Guy have a bit of a problem agreeing on everything, but you love to discuss your differences with someone who also has strong opinions. Taurus admires the way you never let go of your quest to discover the entire truth.

Sexually, Taurus excites you. His raw sensuality inspires you to express yourself physically in your unique way. He'll show his appreciation by stroking all the right areas of your body, while you play his eager, faithful lap dog. Be sure to let him know he's done a great job with one of your electromagnetic orgasms!

You're not the best at keeping house, so show him you're willing to roll up your sleeves and work. He'll appreciate it when you show the same stamina while you're scrubbing as you do in the bedroom, and don't put it past him to ravish you right then and there—before you even have time to put down the mop!

Capricorn

Your friends and family might think the relationship between you and your Taurus Guy is more like a business merger, but you know how wrong they are! You're earthy and practical, but you're also fiery and passionate!

In bed, Taurus responds perfectly to your seduction and feeds on your sexual excitement. Will he get as raw, down, and dirty as you? Absolutely!

You may, however, need to take the bull by the horns, so to speak, when it comes to dividing household chores. Your Taurus Guy is prone to inertia, and unless he's seriously prodded, will want to leave the dirty work up to you. Keep telling him when he's done well, and he'll never leave your side. Remind him how no one scrubs down the kitchen the way he does, and he'll be up and at it in no time. Underneath his staunchly proud exterior there's a really sweet guy who's determined to make you happy.

Aquarius

Your relationship with the Taurus Guy might not make sense to the rest of the world, but they don't know what's going on between the two of you. He adores listening to you talk about your visionary ideas, and you love it when he struggles to find practical solutions to impossible problems.

Your bedroom is a problem-free zone, where the two of you enjoy the wonders of sharing your bodies and strengthening your spiritual connection. His raw sensuality and directness provide a welcome break from the games so many others have played in a ploy to win your heart.

With your Taurus Guy, there are very few questions. You know you can trust him, and he doesn't demand too much from you. He's a what-you-see-is-what-you-get kind of person, and when you're together, your eyes are filled with a vision of pleasure, love, and support that you hope will last a lifetime.

Pisces

Your Taurus Guy is very precious to you. You've finally found someone who knows how to handle life's baffling, practical issues and he adores your creativity and imagination.

In the bedroom, you'll adore being held in his strong arms, and he'll thrill you with his way of making your body tingle all over. He'll like it when you show your appreciation for what he's doing by going all out to make him feel fantastic, too. He's also capable of going to the emotional realm where you truly make love, and may make it there one day, after lots of practice!

The two of you are very different, but as long as you can get him to respect your abilities as much as you are in awe of his, you can have a supremely happy relationship. Keep your self-esteem up by remembering that without your help, your Taurus Guy would be bound to the boring old earth.

YOUR TAURUS GUY AND . . .

Sizing up a relationship with your Taurus Guy involves a lot more than just the two of you. Check this section to find out how you can best make your outside connections, from friends and family to little people and pets, mesh within the patchwork of your steadfast love.

Your Female Friends

Taurus will be very nice to your female friends and try to show off what a great guy he is. He might even cook up one of his "special recipes" to serve to your gal pals when they come over. No matter how hard he tries to hide his insecurity, his secret hope is your friends will rave about him and tell you how lucky you are.

Your Male Friends

The Taurus Guy will pretend he doesn't mind the fact other guys are spending time with you and encroaching on his territory, but a whole different thing is going on inside his head. Expect him to accompany you when he knows you're seeing your guy friends. He won't want to miss out on anything that might go on, and he'll make sure nothing does!

His Female Friends

Taurus attracts female friends by the dozens, not just because he's such a nice guy, but also because he has a softness to him that helps him form instant kinship with the girls. His interests in art, beauty, and food create opportunities for these fun, if innocent, friendships. He'll proudly introduce you to them, and expect you to treat them with respect. If you're jealous, he's hoping you won't show it!

His Male Friends

Taurus, surprisingly, doesn't have a whole lot of male friends. He tends to stick to one or two loyal followers he knows he can trust. He'll have long dinners with these men, usually to talk over their lives, compare notes about finances, or swap tales about the pluses and minuses of their relationships. Let him talk about you, and he'll say only sweet things!

Your Family

Your family is going to love the Taurus Guy because he projects the right combination of material success and emotional maturity. He'll treat them warmly, but keep his distance at first. Taurus has to make sure no one is going to try to swindle him out of money before he'll come closer. If they ply him with great food, and accept him as he is, he'll quickly become part of the furniture.

His Family

The Taurus Guy's relationship with his family is a mixed bag. The relatives could be really nice and supportive, or they could be manipulative and verbally abusive. One thing is for sure: they'll push Taurus to work very hard, and he'll always want them to be proud of him. Help him understand the difference between acceptance and unconditional love, and support him when the rest of the family isn't giving him enough attention.

Your Pets

Taurus likes pets, but would prefer it if someone else were to care for them. He likes pretty animals, such as purebred dogs and cats with fluffy coats and striking hair. If your pet doesn't fit into any of these categories, don't worry. He won't torture your animal; he just won't adore it the way you do.

His Pets

Taurus will look for a pet that is easy to take care of, or he won't have any. He doesn't dislike animals, but he isn't very interested in doing all the dirty work it might take to care for them. He's the kind of guy who prefers horses to small dogs and cats. He loves animals for their natural beauty, especially if they aren't very likely to make a mess in his living quarters.

His Potential for Success

Your friends and family will overwhelmingly approve of the way your Taurus Guy provides a nice lifestyle for you. He always finds great ways to accumulate income, and although he won't sign all of it over to you, his sense of pride will push him to buy you things that allow you to show off how well he treats you. He'll definitely leave you feeling like a very lucky girl.

His Role as a Father

Taurus will want to do everything right when it comes to raising his children. He'll definitely participate in your pregnancy by being a great "coach," but when it's time for the delivery, he could get quite nervous. Over time, he'll build a relationship with the kids that leaves no question in their minds about Dad being the one in charge.

TAURUS COMPATIBILITY

Your Sign	Compatibility Level
Aries	♈♈
Taurus	♉♉♉
Gemini	♊♊
Cancer	♋♋♋♋♋
Leo	♌♌♌♌
Virgo	♍♍♍♍
Libra	♎♎
Scorpio	♏♏♏♏♏
Sagittarius	♐♐
Capricorn	♑♑♑
Aquarius	♒♒♒♒
Pisces	♓♓

SHORT-TERM PROSPECTS

Your Sign	Short-Term Prospects
Aries	♈♈♈♈
Taurus	♉♉♉♉
Gemini	♊♊♊
Cancer	♋♋♋♋♋
Leo	♌♌♌
Virgo	♍♍♍♍
Libra	♎♎
Scorpio	♏♏♏♏♏
Sagittarius	♐♐♐
Capricorn	♑♑♑♑
Aquarius	♒♒♒♒
Pisces	♓♓♓

LONG-TERM PROSPECTS

Your Sign	Long-Term Prospects
Aries	♈
Taurus	♉♉♉
Gemini	♊♊
Cancer	♋♋♋♋
Leo	♌♌♌♌
Virgo	♍♍♍♍
Libra	♎♎
Scorpio	♏♏♏♏♏
Sagittarius	♐♐
Capricorn	♑♑♑♑
Aquarius	♒♒♒♒
Pisces	♓♓

CHAPTER 3

Gemini (May 21–June 20)

YOUR MISSION: Set Him Free, or Pretend to, Anyway

Gemini Potential Pluses

- Talkative
- Open-minded
- Smart
- Savvy
- Inventive
- Friendly
- Adaptable
- Entertaining
- Well connected
- Energetic

Gemini Potential Minuses

- Flirty
- Fickle
- Flighty
- Irresponsible
- Dismissive
- Distracted
- Inattentive
- Forgetful
- Informal
- Unreliable

WHAT THE GEMINI GUY HAS TO GIVE . . .

The Gemini Guy's main purpose in life is to gather and spread information. The appearance of at least two personalities—as embodied in his sign's symbol, the Twins—is a mechanism he uses to attract as many people as possible. Gemini can talk to anyone, any time, and prefers to be in a crowd of people or connected through his computer or handheld device. Yes, he can sometimes split his attention between you and some other person or thought at any given time, but he doesn't do it to insult or upset you: he's a master of multitasking and really is capable of holding at least two conversations in tandem. Being flirty and feverishly thrilled to meet people, he is also capable of loving two people at the same time, albeit in different ways. Some Gemini men have a tendency to cheat because of the intrigue of leading a "double life," but if you tend to his needs and keep him as mentally stimulated as you do sexually, you can build an exciting and enriching relationship.

As a Date:

Gemini will want to test you out as a conversation partner first and foremost, so expect to be taken to a place that's quiet enough for you to chat. If you go to a movie, concert, or show, his compulsion to share his reflections on the evening will probably spill into a romantic café or bistro. He may answer a few phone calls or messages while you're together, so you'll get a glimpse what it would be like to coexist with the network of friends and business connections he's constantly wired into. The Gemini Guy can be really hard to pin down, and the second date might not come right away. In fact, you may have to do some of the pursuing. Always use clever words and original thoughts when you communicate, and he'll be unable to resist calling you back.

As a Sex Partner:

The world of your Gemini Guy consists of his thoughts as much as his deeds. He will love to talk about foreplay, what turns you on, and what gets him excited. He won't jump right into nonverbal communication, but once you demonstrate your skills, he'll gladly succumb and take action. He'll try to remember all the things you told him you liked, but don't hold it against him if he forgets one or two. Gently remind him either with words or by taking the appropriate body part and placing it right where it tingles. As exclusivity isn't something that comes naturally to the Gemini Guy, take care at this stage. Talk about this issue as you evolve from two people on a date and in bed to a couple working out the parameters of your relationship.

As a Domestic Partner:

The Gemini Guy's ability to detach from his emotions will be a big help around the house. He won't fume when something breaks down; he'll quickly think about how he can get someone to fix it. If the problem is electronic or can be solved with a phone call or quick thinking and sweet-talking, he's your man. He's not so eager to help when it comes to manual labor, however. You may have to entice him to do the dirty work by pointing out that while he's using his hands he can keep his mind occupied by thinking about using his network of friends to get ahead in the world. Add a few statistics about incubation and the creative process, and before you know it, he'll extol the virtues of using his precious time to scrub floors and rake leaves.

Emotionally:

Just because your Gemini Guy tends to intellectualize his feelings doesn't mean he hasn't got them. In fact, because he sublimates them, he often acts on them without being conscious that's what he's doing. He's exceptionally good at arguing, and he'll use his intellect and talent for turning words to persuade you to think you were wrong and he deserves an apology. When you hurt his feelings, he'll try not to show it. Instead, he'll avoid spending time with you and maybe further entrench himself in some of his social networking activities. Gemini doesn't need to be inspired or motivated to cheat or flirt, but when he is wounded, his tendency to stray will come out stronger than ever. You and your Gemini Guy can keep harmony in your relationship by talking through your feelings and keeping the lines of communication permanently open.

FIND YOUR GEMINI GUY!

Like the planet that rules him and the metal that shares its name—Mercury—your Gemini Guy isn't easy to catch or contain. If you threaten his freedom in any way, he'll run in the opposite direction.

Making him *want* to be with you can entail everything from letting him bounce his many ideas around with you and listening to repeat renditions of his favorite stories, even if you'd often rather be somewhere else. If you can show this kind of devotion to your Gemini Guy while also being willing to let him roam free, he'll return to you and your relationship like a happily contented boomerang.

No one can blame you for being attracted to the Gemini Guy! Read on to see how you can use the attributes of your sign to lure him closer and get him hooked on you!

Aries

The Gemini Guy will impress you with the way he knows exactly what to say to people, especially you. He'll probably compliment you on your physical strength or notice how fiercely independent you are.

This latter attribute is the one that he will find most attractive. He will like the idea that you can stand on your own while he goes about his business.

When you're together, he'll probably talk more than you would like. You can always quiet him down by practicing the art of seduction. How can he *not* forget about whatever is on his mind when you lay one of your passionate, unforgettable kisses on him?

When he gets angry, runs off, or flirts with someone else, don't start a war. The more you can play the game of not caring about what he does, the faster he'll run back into your arms.

Taurus

You and the Gemini Guy have two distinct ways of looking at life, and your mutual curiosity will definitely draw you together. He'll enjoy being around someone who's totally reliable and predictable, and you'll be intrigued by the way he pops in and out of your life. You'll rise to the challenge of keeping him coming back to you, but first you need to learn more about what that will entail.

The Gemini Guy likes variety and stimulation, and for him to get it, there will have to be times when you are not together. Build up trust in him by watching how he comes back, even when it seems as though he was off flirting with someone else. Don't be afraid to call him, but when you do, take a clever and engaging tone. He'll balk at the first hint of possessiveness. You'll both have to work hard to be together, but the things you learn from one another will be very much worth your trouble.

Gemini

What will happen when you meet a fellow Gemini? You'll be intensely attracted to each other, but you will always struggle to stay together as a couple because both of you will resist the idea of being tied to one person at a time.

If you want to be in a lasting, loving relationship, however, you're going to have to work through this issue together. Make little tests for yourselves to prove you're getting ready to make a commitment. On weekends, go away together, where very few other people are around. When you get closer emotionally as well as physically, you'll begin to find reasons to abandon your flirtations and fleeting glances at others. Not the least of your reasons to stay with a Gemini Guy: you can produce fantastic ideas when you put your heads together!

Cancer

You'll be enticed by the Gemini Guy's fresh outlook on life and feel very flattered when he singles you out for his attention; however, there are things you need to know before you assume he's the man of your dreams.

He doesn't like to be tied down to one person, and he can be very hard to get to know. It's not that he doesn't like you: it's more that he worries about what being with someone as sensitive and caring as you is going to entail. He's concerned he won't measure up to your standards, especially if you want someone who'll be there for you no matter what.

In order to calm him down and let him know you won't smother him with your love, you'll have to let him roam when he wants. He may even date several other women while he's getting to know you. When you show him you're the one who'll understand him, support his ideas, and take care of his physical, sexual, and emotional needs, he'll come to realize he's already found the right one to come home to—*you*!

Leo

You and your Gemini Guy will have a great friendship, right from the moment you lay eyes on each other. It's likely that you'll meet in a crowded place because you both love people. While you're no amateur at attracting attention—usually by dramatizing stories and mesmerizing your audience—you'll marvel at the way he works a room. He'll be all over the place, shaking hands and making friends with everyone present.

He'll love the way you command attention with your magnetic presence and jovial manner. He'll also appreciate it when you offer pointers on how he can be even more effective in his work and when you hear out his groundbreaking ideas. Make it clear to him, though, that you need a certain amount of attention and that, as long as you get it, you'll be happy to let him go out into the world to collect and spread as much information as he can process.

Virgo

The Gemini Guy's conversation skills will amaze you. He'll make it seem as though you've known him all your life within the first few moments. His cool, attractive exterior will draw you in, too, and although you'll see right through his charm, it will still endear him to you.

The two of you share Mercury as the planet ruler of your signs, so you understand why it's so important for him to take everything that happens and try to put it into words. Like him, you tend to analyze the world around you, and he admires the way you organize your thoughts and use logic to solve practical problems. When you're together, you'll realize the possibility of making true magic.

It's clear you'll have a lot to talk about, but don't neglect to make time for fun. He's flexible and likes to be spontaneous. You already know you need to let Gemini roam around, but make it clear when you want a commitment. It won't take him long to figure out what's good for him!

Libra

It's easy for you to like the Gemini Guy. Just like you, he uses his mind to take in the people and places around him, and the two of you can have long and lovely conversations together. You admire his ability to find something to talk about with everyone he comes across, and you marvel at the way he remembers facts and figures. His mentally active nature stimulates you, and you love the way he makes you think.

Your diplomatic skills impress him, and he'll often ask you what you think is the right thing to say to someone. He will also sense that you need almost constant reassurance about how beautiful you are, and he'll provide it . . . when he's around. The one tough thing about being with a Gemini Guy will be the way he isn't always right by your side. You'll have to let him loose now and then and trust that he'll come back to you, no matter how flirty he seems, because you're the one who can show him complete, true love.

Scorpio

The Gemini Guy will really challenge you, and that will be much of the attraction. His elusive, here-now-not-here style will keep you wondering what you have to do in order to catch this attractive, talkative lad.

You'll probably meet him because he strikes up a conversation with you. You'll be attracted to his finely honed communication skills, and his broad knowledge of the world will amaze you. Before long, you'll perceive the ultimate truth about keeping this one around: he needs to know you're strong and secure enough to set him free!

He'll love the way you seem to cut right through any sort of illusion, but he'll be slightly afraid of what you'll ask of him should your relationship progress beyond casual dating. If you want to go forward, you'll have to work hard at learning to let go. With luck, your Gemini Guy will show you why he's worth it.

Sagittarius

Were those birds you heard singing when the Gemini Guy came up to you and said "hello"? It could seem like a totally magic moment when the two of you first meet. He has all the things you love in a guy—from an impish and clever way of expressing himself to the ability to hold his own without expecting you to provide all the support and entertainment he seems to require.

You'll make a big impression on him when you tell him about your adventures, and admit that, just like him, you're not crazy about the idea of making commitments. Eventually, as the two of you begin to trust in your mutual autonomy, the magic of love can take over and create the kind of relationship only two people who were made for each other can hope for.

Capricorn

Your first impression of the Gemini Guy will probably awaken that cynical side of your sense of humor. The cute jokes he makes to get your attention may not make you swoon, but he'll be able to show you he's willing to impress you. A natural born salesman, he won't take long to have even you convinced that he's the one you've been waiting for.

He'll be in awe of your ability to manage and command leadership. He'll look to you to tell him what's proper and traditional, and you'll help him learn how to avoid offending people by failing to keep his word. With a Gemini, it's important to avoid doing all this with too heavy a hand, however. Even if you get him to stay on an imaginary leash, he'll never walk to heel! You'll have to give him plenty of rope, and hope he comes back to you before doing himself any real harm.

Aquarius

The Gemini Guy has a certain way of expressing himself that makes it almost impossible for you to avoid bursting out into a megawatt smile. His freewheeling style and obvious talent for getting people to listen to what he has to say evoke your admiration, and you'll also like his ease with all things technological.

He'll like the way you share with him a desire to move forward into a future where the problems and restrictions that hold people back no longer exist. Indeed, the Gemini Guy can get lost in the world of ideas with you, but what you'll like best is the way you have such an easy time playing together. You share interests in the same kinds of quirky movies and TV shows, and he'll admire your socially conscious activities. The one problem you might have is finding enough time for each other. Stay involved in one another's daily lives, and your two-peas-in-a-pod-type friendship will grow into a lasting, heavenly love.

Pisces

The Gemini Guy will appeal to you right away because he doesn't go for all the rigid rules and restrictions so many other people insist you conform to. Like you, he's flexible, and enjoys the way you go with the flow. His ideas about commitment match yours, in that you'd rather not jump into anything too serious.

He'll appreciate how you accept him as he is and don't pressure him to tell you every detail of his daily comings and goings. He'll also deeply admire your imagination and possibly collaborate with you when you come up with an idea or story that he just knows the rest of the world would love to hear. You'll have a great deal of fun together and view life as one big adventure to be enjoyed. You might put off formally making a commitment, but your kind of love will make it abundantly clear that life is just more fun when the two of you are together.

KEEP YOUR GEMINI GUY!

Once your Gemini Guy gets used to the idea of being in a committed relationship, how do you keep him coming home? You'll have to think as fast as he does and supply a never-ending stream of entertainment for him. While he enjoys having his own schedule to keep, he'll really love it when the two of you, as a couple, have a fully booked "dance card." The only thing he likes more than accepting invites is saying "no" to them when he's simply too busy.

His flirtatious ways will probably never go away, so you have to understand what his dalliances mean to him . . . *nothing*! He merely wants to use his powers of attraction to meet people and learn more about them. If you notice, he even has a way of talking to other men that involves catering to their interests and needs. He's a shape-shifter, but always eager to please, especially when it comes to you.

The rewards of staying with your Gemini Guy for the long haul are many, but you'll get at them faster by understanding how the two of you mix. Check for your sign below to learn more about creating a safe space for you and your Gemini Guy to have a happy, sustained relationship.

Aries

You will always be on the go, you and your Gemini Guy, because you both thrive on stimulation. You're not as interested in the intellectual stuff in which he immerses himself, and he's not all that physically inclined. Maybe after he goes to his Mensa meeting and you get done playing in your soccer league, the two of you can get together for what really matters.

Your sex life will be rich and rewarding because you each appreciate what the other has to offer. While most women would merely hope he raises his eyes from that handheld or video game long enough to notice you're trying to seduce him, you'll move right in for the "kill." Meanwhile, he'll have all kinds of ideas he's picked up from talking to his buddies about making it all worth your while.

When two people are determined to impress one another, as you both are, you'll put all your considerable energy into making your relationship last.

Taurus

As your relationship with your Gemini Guy progresses, give him his space while still being satisfied with the time you have together, and you'll see that your effort will pay off.

Squeezing "quality" out of your dates and down time will entail getting his nose out of his electronic devices and into your face. There will also be times when he wants you to pay more attention to him and stop poring over work stuff or your joint finances. The best thing each of you can do is focus on the reasons why you're together rather than paying too much attention to the world around you.

He loves you for your stability, and you love him for his unpredictability. The two of you can really enjoy one another when you build or plan something together. You'll also have to gather enough faith in your relationship to believe that no matter how many other people he talks with in a day, he's saving up his most intense and loving moments for you.

Gemini

The two of you might need to hire a referee in order to negotiate who will be talking at any given time. There are times when silence from both of you will be most appropriate, especially when it comes to your intimate relations.

In bed, you and your fellow Gemini will talk through what you want to do in order to please one another, which is great. It will be even better when the two of you actually do these things! Take the lead and tell him to "shush" while you proceed to work on his body with your talented hands. He'll know what to do almost immediately, and before you know it, the two of you will be champions at lovemaking!

Your mutual interest in endless variety will make it easier to stick together. Even if you both keep flirting, you won't stray. How could you not see that, in truth, there's no one else you'd rather be with than your very best friend?

Cancer

You and your Gemini Guy will love being together, but you'll each have your own challenges. He'll have to learn about you before you can become really comfortable with him. He'll be away from home a lot, so your job is to come to believe he isn't looking for anyone else.

The best way to kill two birds with one stone: do your learning in bed! Turn off all the electronics and show him some old-fashioned sexual electricity. He'll come to realize that your deep sensitivity and ability to determine what's going to turn him on before he thinks of it will be hard to replace. Show him the wildcat that runs wild within you, and he'll convince you that no matter who he meets, he'll always come home to you.

Love will flow in both directions in your relationship, but you'll have to learn how to recognize it. Although he may not spend most of his time on one knee begging for your devotion, he'll let you know he's yours. Make sure you're not so busy making demands on him that you miss the whole thing.

Leo

Your Gemini Guy will continue to dazzle you, even after you decide to make your relationship more than a casual thing. His intellect and his way with people will impress you, and you'll be very proud to be the one he's chosen to be with . . . most of the time. It's important for you to keep an independent life going while you're with Gemini because, for him, the freedom to go out among his other friends is mandatory.

That's why the time you spend in bed together is so special. By being the incredible sex goddess you are, you can give Gemini every reason to come home earlier than he originally planned. You'll also benefit from knowing he's out there bragging about how good he has it at home.

As long as you can recognize his kind of devotion, you and your Gemini Guy can be very happy. Remember to honor his independence, and surround yourself with friends and family to visit with until he comes back home again.

Virgo

The Gemini Guy will be a very satisfying love match for you. There's a lot to learn from him, and he's open to listening to your suggestions, too. Both of you are very capable of taking care of yourselves, but you realize that by being together you can build a life that's bigger and better than anything you could create all on your own.

In bed, Gemini will be very impressed with the way you seem to read what he wants and get right down to the business of making him happy. Lavish every last technique you know on him: he never tires of variety!

Let him offer you the pleasure of knowing he's looking for ways to please you, and you'll see that although he doesn't always seem to be singularly devoted to your relationship, he's definitely intent on keeping you around. With flexibility and enough love, the two of you will last for much longer than you ever imagined.

Libra

There's a lot to be said for life with your Gemini Guy. He understands the way you see life, and like you, tends to intellectualize most of the things that bog others down in negative emotions. It's easy to explain yourselves to one another.

In bed, there will be no need for either of you to explain a thing. You might be the one person who can get Gemini to stop talking, at least for a little while. The way you look and how you come on to him will leave him speechless, while he scrambles to find ways to touch and tantalize you that will make him feel worthy of being in your presence.

Your aura of beauty and grace will keep Gemini coming back, along with the instant friendship you struck up the moment you met. No matter how many other people he gets to know while he's out there networking, his heart will always be tuned into you.

Scorpio

For you and your Gemini Guy, your deep sense of purpose and his intense curiosity will keep you together. You need to show him that the Scorpion in you doesn't want to smother or overcome him; he wants to demonstrate that he can be devoted to you while retaining his individuality.

You can practice coexisting and learn more about each other while you're having sex. He'll spend a lot of time telling you what will make him feel loved, satisfied, and satiated—and plenty of time asking you what you want. When he shows his willingness to please, you can appreciate who he already is instead of trying to transform him into the man you want him to be.

Live and let live is a great adage to build a relationship by. When you and your Gemini Guy get into the rhythm of your togetherness, you'll be glad you're learning how to love and let go all at the same time.

Sagittarius

Being with your Gemini Guy is like a dream, because you probably didn't think you would ever get a chance to love someone who would be willing to let you be who you are and do what pleases you.

With Gemini, you have someone who not only appreciates his independence, but also enjoys going on adventures with you. Because you both are always seeking out information, you'll enjoy traveling, especially when you get to have great sex in so many unusual places!

In bed, you'll know exactly what to do for one another because you'll talk it through. You might also want to encourage him to release his more animalistic nature so he can more fully enjoy the things that turn both of you on.

This relationship is the kind that can last a very long time, as long as you remain realistic about your expectations and find a level of commitment that keeps you together just enough to help you remain happily ensconced in couplehood.

Capricorn

Although there will be times when you find your Gemini Guy's flightiness to be infuriating, on the whole you'll see your life together as enriching and enlightening. He will help you see the benefit of taking care of yourself in the same way you try to provide for others, while you provide sexual sensations that he's never felt before.

In bed, you'll take the lead. Gemini lives in his head and doesn't always spend enough time thinking of ways to dive into sexual pleasure. You, on the other hand, recognize sex as your way of validating your earthly existence and will teach him the secrets of carnal bliss.

The exchange between the two of you might not be what you always hoped for in a relationship, but it'll open doors to a new world, where you learn how to be more adaptable and where he becomes more organized and reliable.

Aquarius

You and your Gemini Guy know that both of you have made a very lucky find! You'll love the way he seems so in-tune with everything you do, and he'll love you for your independence and vision.

In bed, the two of you will need a bit of warming up. Because you like to talk so much, you might think the physical part of your relationship isn't that important. Not so! The more you relate on a nonverbal level, the stronger your bond will be. The communication you achieve on the sexual level will give you every reason to spend more time in the same place.

While you can both be busy individuals, it's important to put time into your life as a couple. Take the initiative when you have to, and plan for weekends away or nights of wild passion right in your own bedroom. Your Gemini Guy thrives on sexy surprises!

Pisces

You and your Gemini Guy will find it pretty easy to get along. Even though you're way more emotionally oriented than he is, his wide-open mind permits him to understand where you're coming from. He'll do all he can to be sensitive to your needs, but you'll also have to accept his ability to pay attention to something or someone else and love you all at the same time.

Your sex life is the area where you'll notice how close you really are. You and your Gemini Guy will be open to making love at any time and in many different places. You feed on one another's strengths and buttress one another against the rest of the world, despite your weaknesses.

The thing that you each share is a willingness to love one another. It isn't easy for either of you to make a full commitment, but if you jump right in and take a leap of faith you'll find that before long, you won't want to imagine life without him!

YOUR GEMINI GUY AND . . .

Sizing up the Gemini Guy gets easier when you understand how he interacts with the key people in life, both his and yours! Read on to get an idea of what the Gemini Guy is capable of, and what being with him might bring to your other relationships.

Your Female Friends

It would probably be a good idea to stay very close to your Gemini Guy when he's around your friends. Leaving him alone in any place with a lot of women would be just like leaving a kid alone in a candy store. He doesn't mean to hurt you, but when you're not around, he'll have trouble holding back the automatic reflex he has to flirt with anyone he can!

Your Male Friends

The Gemini Guy will be okay with your male friends, or at least he'll pretend to be. He might even use your spending time with them as a shield, pointing out that if you can hang out with them, you shouldn't be so sensitive about him hanging out with female friends. They can be yours or his—it doesn't matter to him as long as he gets to try out his flirting skills on the girls.

His Female Friends

Don't be surprised that your Gemini Guy is inundated with female friends. He's flirty, cute, and savvy, and he has all these neat gadgets he's always flashing around. For the most part, these friendships will be quite innocent. But, as with most men, you always have to wonder whether something less innocuous is in the back of his mind. If you simply go out with him when he meets them, you'll probably feel lots better.

His Male Friends

Your Gemini Guy does have some other men he hangs around with from time to time, but they will rarely be the focus of his life. He usually finds they don't want to talk nearly as much as he does, or as much as you or his female friends might. Also, Gemini really does like to talk to strangers more than anyone. Isn't that most likely the way that he met you?

Your Family

He's a great talker, and your family will immediately see what you see in him: how absolutely clever he is! As crazy as he might be about you, though, being with your family can make him uncomfortable, especially in the early days of your relationship. Take things slowly, and let him get his feet wet gradually. Before long he'll be participating in the family board game tournaments and wearing goofy reunion T-shirts along with the rest of the clan.

His Family

He's good friends with most of the people in his family, but not necessarily a stickler for tradition or large gatherings where there's too much noise for any type of real conversation. He'll enjoy introducing you, but probably not during the first weeks of your time together. When he does, that's a sure sign that he's inching ever so slowly in the direction of making some sort of commitment.

Your Pets

He'll always be good to pets! These creatures, although they don't usually talk, do hold a lot of appeal to the Gemini Guy. He finds them to be a steadying kind of force and likes to watch you interact with them. He'll slowly come to take them on as his own, but just like anything else that smacks of getting tied down, not too much too soon.

His Pets

He likes pets, but maybe more when they belong to other people. To the Gemini Guy, they're a blessing and a curse. He wouldn't be able to stand having to leave a happy hour or party to go home and feed or walk the cat or dog. However, when it comes to making connections to other happy pet owners, he'll be all about his furry friends.

His Potential for Success

The Gemini Guy can be a very good earner, but he's also a big spender. To him, there can never be enough "toys," so he keeps buying them—for himself! This is okay when he has more than enough money to spare, but when funds run short for the bare necessities, and he's busily playing with the latest techno-gadget wistfully in the corner, it's probably gone too far.

His Role as a Father

The Gemini Dad will be best buddies with his kids, and he'll read and tell stories to them. He'll be the perfect parent when it comes to taking them places or dropping off and picking up at the school. Tell him to be careful, though: he can get all wrapped up in conversations with the other parents and teachers—and leave the kid there waiting, nervously clutching an empty lunch bag!

GEMINI COMPATIBILITY

Your Sign	Compatibility Level
Aries	♈♈♈
Taurus	♉♉
Gemini	♊♊♊♊
Cancer	♋♋
Leo	♌♌♌
Virgo	♍♍♍♍
Libra	♎♎♎♎
Scorpio	♏
Sagittarius	♐♐♐♐♐
Capricorn	♑♑♑
Aquarius	♒♒♒♒
Pisces	♓♓♓♓

GEMINI SHORT-TERM PROSPECTS

Your Sign	Short-Term Prospects
Aries	♈♈♈♈
Taurus	♉♉
Gemini	♊♊♊♊♊
Cancer	♋
Leo	♌♌♌
Virgo	♍♍
Libra	♎♎♎
Scorpio	♏♏
Sagittarius	♐♐♐♐
Capricorn	♑♑♑
Aquarius	♒♒♒♒♒
Pisces	♓♓

GEMINI LONG-TERM PROSPECTS

Your Sign	Long-Term Prospects
Aries	♈♈♈
Taurus	♉♉
Gemini	♊♊♊
Cancer	♋♋
Leo	♌♌
Virgo	♍♍♍
Libra	♎♎♎♎
Scorpio	♏
Sagittarius	♐♐♐♐
Capricorn	♑♑♑
Aquarius	♒♒♒♒♒
Pisces	♓♓♓♓

CHAPTER 4

Cancer (June 21–July 21)

YOUR MISSION: Let Him Nurture You

Cancer Potential Pluses

- Caring
- Compassionate
- Domestic
- Emotional
- Resourceful
- Nurturing
- Gentle
- Protective
- Tenacious
- Traditional

Cancer Potential Minuses

- Cranky
- Moody
- Possessive
- Clinging
- Manipulative
- Irrational
- Prudish
- Volatile
- Unfocused
- Withholding

WHAT THE CANCER GUY HAS TO GIVE . . .

Sweet, kind, and gushing with emotion, the Cancer Guy has some unusual attributes. He's quite capable of showing his manliness, sexually as well as socially, yet there are things about him that remind you of someone you know—most likely your mom! He'll nurture you and love you and coddle you . . . and probably pressure you to have kids long before you think you're ready! For Cancer, the act of taking care of another person gives him a sense of purpose. His moods will vary much in the way his sign's ruler, the Moon, changes its appearance from night to night. Also, his sign's symbol, the Crab, speaks to Cancer's desire to protect himself and those he loves. The Crab also depicts his tenacious qualities. Once he has you in his grip, he'll put up the fight of his life before he'll let go! It will be all right, though. There are worse things that can happen to you than being loved by this caring, serious, and sensitive man!

As a Date:

From the outset, Cancer will want to know what you like and go to great lengths to make sure he obtains it for you. He'll want to talk to you a lot, but you'll also notice his tendency to get physically, if innocently, close to you. Holding hands and looking into your eyes are his ways of finding out if there's a potential for you to be together beyond a date or two. If he takes you out to eat, you'll be in for a treat. Cancer has a knack for finding great restaurants! His affinity for food is so strong, in fact, that he may even enjoy cooking you a meal while you discuss your basic likes, dislikes, and reasons you'd like to be together. Cancer will tend to bond with you even before you've decided you're interested in him, so tread lightly! Don't promise more than you intend to deliver.

As a Sex Partner:

The act of sex is a sacred rite to the Cancer Guy. He lays his emotions out bare to you, as he offers his heart, mind, and soul along with his body. You might have to wait awhile for him to get to the kind of aggressive action you'd expect from the average male, but once he gets started, his potency can be quite astounding. After all, the ultimate goal for the Cancer Guy is to have someone to take care of, and if he's ever going to procreate, he figures he'd best give it his best shot, so to speak. He loves coddling you, of course, but rocking his very own baby in his arms is never too far from the forefront of his mind. Until the real child comes, he'll be more than glad to cater to you and ensure he keeps you happy and content.

As a Life Partner:

The Cancer Guy is quite domestic, but for the most part his caretaking skills will be centered on you in the bedroom and on anybody who's the slightest bit hungry in the kitchen! Even if he's not a cook, he'll know where you can get the most sumptuous meals, and ensure you're getting all you need to nurture your body, mind, and soul. He's a good provider, in that he won't allow you to go without; however, when given the choice between hours at the office and little time at home, he'll opt for less money and more family time. Cleaning isn't his forte, but he'll help if you ask him to. In general, the Cancer Guy will do what it takes to make you happy because he feels it's his job to keep a smile on your face.

Emotionally:

The Cancer Guy bonds to his partner and holds on for dear life. If you don't like getting phone calls in the middle of the day enquiring about your health, you'll need to tell him you can't talk to him from work. Cancer's tendency to hover and smother you with love can be comforting, but after a point it can also become annoying. He'll understand it if you want him to lay off, but that probably won't happen before his feelings are deeply hurt. This man—who is sensitive enough to know what you want before you do—is also vulnerable enough to be very wounded by the slightest sign of your disapproval. You must tread very softly if you don't want to crush Cancer's ego and send him off to retreat into his shell.

FIND YOUR CANCER GUY!

Before you invite the Cancer Guy to love you, make sure you're prepared to have him stick around for a very long while! Just like a doting parent, he'll love you almost no matter what, and he'll try everything there is to do before he gives up on your relationship. Once you decide you want him, it's fairly easy to get him. Let him know you need him to take care of you. This feeds right into his sense of purpose and will send him straight into your arms! Act surprised when he does wonderful things for you, and show your appreciation openly. That's all you need to do to keep him with you forever.

The Cancer Guy can be quite a catch, so obtain the advantages you need by reading for your sign below. Soon you'll know how to decode his moods and get him to turn all that love and nurturing your way.

Aries

Meeting Cancer will be easy because he'll be the one trying to appeal to your sense of being in need of adult supervision. You'll identify his ability to take care of you emotionally as well as physically, and you'll willingly do just enough of a role reversal to protect him from people who play too rough for his liking. You'll love the way he takes care of you so you can be strong enough to face the world; he'll love your courage and appreciate the way you can make decisions quickly and without a big production.

Be careful about losing your temper around your Cancer Guy, though. The sensitivity you so greatly admire about him can also lead him to go into a deep, brooding state of mind that will make it seem as though your love has been destroyed. You won't want that to happen!

Taurus

You and the Cancer Guy will have a very easy time getting along. He'll pick up your need to keep things slow and sane from the get-go. He'll ply you with food and listen to stories about your childhood with rapt attention. He'll also share his past with you, hoping you'll find the same level of fascination with his childhood he does.

He'll love your predictability, but at times he'll want you to branch out and try some different things. He might like your favorite restaurant, for example, but he'll hope you'll be open to trying a few of his.

Your tendency to be unmovable once you form an opinion could cause some difficulty with your Cancer Guy. He'll want you to be able to change your mind without feeling as though you're giving up your autonomy. He'll also try to show you it's safe to make changes and encourage you to feel confident, even when you don't know exactly what's going to happen from moment to moment.

Gemini

You'll recognize the Cancer Guy right away, because in some sense, he's the answer to your wildest nightmare. This guy wants to settle down as soon as possible, while you would much rather be free to make absolutely sure you've found the right person. In another way, though, he can be your dream guy. Here is someone who can offer the secure home base you can rely on, along with unconditional love, reliable assistance and support, and just about the perfect set of attributes for your future family.

Before you allow him to pull you away with one pincher into his cozy cove, make sure you're aware of his need to be almost constantly reassured. Your flirtations with others will drive him crazy, and although he may struggle to avoid letting you see it, the suffering he endures can ultimately destroy his trust in you. Be open and honest with your Cancer Guy, and make sure he knows how much you value his love and attention.

Cancer

The Cancer Guy's quiet manner will be a relief for you, and you'll like the way he doesn't push you into things, from partying at wild clubs to eating foods that upset your stomach.

He'll love how well you take care of him, but he'll also want you to learn to let him take care of you. Although this would be easy for most people, for you it isn't. You can trust the Cancer Guy, though, and even if he doesn't seem to be strong or domineering, he's exceptionally protective.

Your relationship will go well as long as you're willing to share the caretaking duties. There will be times when you're the one who's in a better position to take care of him, while there will be other moments that call for him to tend to you and your needs. No one is "better" or "worse" for being the one on the receiving end! Let him love you, and you'll experience happiness you never even dreamed of.

Leo

You'll admire the Cancer Guy because his sensitivity gives him an uncanny ability to read other people. His ability to anticipate your needs, in particular, will endear him to you. You realize it takes a strong person to defer his own pleasure so someone else can be just a little bit happier.

He'll be in awe of your ability to stand up and speak your truth, and he'll appreciate it when you point out ways that he can become stronger and more courageous about taking on life's challenges. Take care though—because you can be somewhat bold and brassy, you'll have to moderate your choice of words and the tone you use. He can be very sensitive, especially if he believes you think he's your inferior.

The two of you have a lot to exchange. His nurturing energy and your encouraging spirit will combine to make both of you better people. You'll cheer each other on as you push one another on to your greatest potential.

Virgo

You'll be sweet on the Cancer Guy from the moment he walks up to you. He'll probably show you right away that he's capable of looking after you. His kindness and empathy will mesh very well with your own need to take care of others and make sure they have everything they need.

Perhaps one of the things you'll like most about him is his willingness to ask you for help in organizing his life. Most guys will act as though they have it all together when they don't; the Cancer Guy will admit his weaknesses and, by doing so, will show off his strengths.

You'll have to soft-pedal your criticisms of his way of doing things, though. His sensitivity makes it almost impossible for him to hear negative comments as anything but attacks. Explain your motivation—to help him out—and he'll be way more receptive. Once you work out the best ways of communicating to one another, this relationship has great staying power and genuine potential.

Libra

You'll be very attracted to the Cancer Guy because you'll fall in love with the way he seems to want to take care of all the things you'd rather not bother with. This includes cooking, maybe some cleaning, and definitely listening to your problems and helping you organize your life.

He'll be in awe of your beauty and be willing to help you because he knows you'll appreciate him. Nonetheless, there are limits to his tolerance, and if he detects you're being lazy, he'll stop taking care of you until you pick up your share of the heavy lifting. Before you get serious, make sure you also realize how sensitive he can be. He'll be willing to hear you out when you're not happy with the way things are going, but if he thinks you're criticizing him, he'll be deeply wounded. If this happens, simply take him in your arms and let him know that it's okay to let you love and support him, too.

Scorpio

The Cancer Guy is a lot like you, so you'll pick up on his sensitivity and be attracted to him right away. His soulful eyes and gentle voice will soothe you, and even though he might not be the strongest and bravest man you've met, you will love how he resonates with your deep, emotional way of being.

He'll adore it when you take control of the situation and do all you can to protect and defend your territory. Be careful about showing him too much of your vengeful side, though: until he knows you well enough to realize you would never hurt him, you could scare him off.

The two of you will rock on a sea of emotion, and you'll enjoy being as protective of your Cancer Guy as he is of you. Together, you laugh in the faces of those who have no idea about what it means to love with their entire beings, the way you do.

Sagittarius

The ultrasensitive Cancer Guy seems like an unlikely match for you, but in truth you can get along really well. He'll show his sensitivity right off the bat, so look him in the eye and convince him that— no matter how brave and bold you are—you just don't have it in you to intentionally hurt anyone.

Once you've gained his trust, he'll come to admire your innocence and will begin to take care of you in little ways. Don't balk when he wipes your mouth or points out that piece of spinach you have stuck in your teeth. He knows you want to look your best and doesn't mean to criticize.

Although he can seem to threaten your freedom, he doesn't mean to. He will want a lot of attention, though, so make him slow down if your lives begin to enmesh at a pace that makes you uncomfortable. It's best to let your relationship with the Cancer Guy ripen at the exact, perfect rate!

Capricorn

When you meet the Cancer Guy, you might immediately sense you've come across the perfect guy for you. While you're detached and serious, he's extremely attentive and gushy. Rather than wanting to run away because he wants to take care of you, it's easy to feel attracted to him and the kind of life he has to offer.

He'll love the way you have your life arranged and admire your ability to organize and lead other people. He'll want you to let him fuss over you, so don't feel bashful about giving him a chance to take care of your every need.

Your relationship might seem like an interesting twist on the typical male-female arrangement, but that doesn't mean it can't work. As long as you're willing to be the "strong one" and he accepts a supporting role without feeling like his manhood is being neutered, the two of you can build on your strengths and create a fabulously fulfilling relationship.

Aquarius

The Cancer Guy will approach you because he'll wonder what he can do to make you feel comfortable, as though he senses your feeling of being separate from the average crowd. You'll love the way he can pick up on your feelings without you having to say a word about them, but be prepared: this can also spook *you* to some degree. You can ask him to be less honest about what he senses from you, but that won't be easy for him.

He'll admire your coolness and composure and will envy the way you can detach when someone takes an action that would hurt your feelings. You'll find that he's devastated when someone criticizes him, and this could put you off at first.

Once you get to know him, though, you'll see how much he has to offer. As long as you can instruct him to avoid becoming possessive and/or clingy, you'll enjoy being coddled and cared for by the most nurturing man you've met.

Pisces

Meeting the Cancer Guy will be like a breath of fresh air because at last you will have found a man who feels his emotions as deeply as you do. He'll sense your moods, and gladly listen when you need someone to talk to.

He'll love the way you can just go with your imagination and wind up living in a world that's filled with magic and joy. He'll also appreciate your undying love for the world and share your empathy for people who are less fortunate than either of you are.

Sometimes, he might seem clingier than you'd like. Teach him that you need to be alone from time to time so you can connect with the fantasy world he enjoys sharing with you so much. It won't be hard for him to keep his distance when he knows it's something you want. It's hard to imagine anyone who wants to please you more than the Cancer Guy.

KEEP YOUR CANCER GUY!

By the time you're sure about your relationship with your Cancer Guy, he probably already has your china pattern all picked out! This traditional, family-oriented man is usually looking to settle down as soon as possible, but don't let him rush you. Make sure you know you have the same values and that you're able to be sensitive enough to him to avoid crushing his feelings with a single word.

Staying with your Cancer Guy will also mean being open to allowing him to care for you. If you're the utterly independent type, this could mean a substantial departure from your instincts. He'll insist on doing certain things for you, and it will feel good to have him take care of you. If you're sensing there are strings attached, though, you're probably on the right track . . . but all he asks is your love and devotion in return.

It might seem easy to get used to living under the love and care of the Cancer Guy, but staying together can be a whole other thing. Read on to see how you can use the characteristics of your sign to keep those home-cooked meals and TLC-laced nights coming your way.

Aries

Life with your Cancer Guy will be filled with love, and you'll adore the way he's always there to listen to your news and share in your triumphs and defeats. He'll be very proud of you and pleased that you enjoy letting him pamper you with the right food, extra blankets when you need them, and a smile when you're feeling down.

In bed, the two of you will have a wonderful time. Your Cancer Guy will show you the value of taking your time to show your emotion, as he unveils all he has to offer by looking ever so deeply into your eyes.

You'll have an instant domestic engineer on your hands in your Cancer Guy, but don't get upset when he wants you to do your part. After all, you'll have a hard time finding anyone else who can make you feel as loved and cared for as your Cancer Guy does, anywhere in the universe.

Taurus

Enjoying comfort and softness as much as you do, the calm, reassuring touch of your Cancer Guy will relax you and make you happy to be with him. He'll be grateful to you for appreciating him and for helping him stand up to people who try to take advantage of him.

In bed, you'll adore being seen-to by this man: he won't stop trying to please you until you ache from the intensity of your orgasms. In turn, when you bring him to the height of sexual ecstasy, he'll be lost in the sea of emotions in which he spends most of his time.

When you disagree, try not to bully your Cancer Guy. Not only is he tremendously sensitive: he remembers everything you say and do. If he brings up one of your less thoughtful comments during some future fight, you'll wish you'd remembered to tread more lightly with this delicate man.

Gemini

You and your Cancer Guy will have more in common than you think. Even though he's much more tied to things such as home and family than you are, he also enjoys talking, mostly about his feelings. He loves listening to your stories and delights in meeting your many friends.

Your ability to converse with your Cancer Guy will really come in handy when you go to bed. Listen to what he says about his feelings, but also learn to pick up on them from the things he does with his body. His eyes will almost always show what he's feeling inside, and because he's the type of guy who'd rather show love through action than words. You'll like that, for sure!

You'll have to practice being more attentive and caring than you might think you need to be while you're with your Cancer Guy, but he'll pay you back by always being there to take care of you when you're so stressed out you don't know what to do next.

Cancer

Both you and your Cancer Guy enjoy the domestic life, and after you get together, you might very rarely go out. Still, you can be happy that way, so don't worry about it! In fact, remember that you and your Cancer Guy can both get lost in thinking too much about what could go wrong: The two of you find it easy to always be planning for "the worst," but if you try instead to consider what it would be like to enjoy "the best," you'll be way happier.

It'll be important for the two of you to keep your mood swings in synch, but because you're both so sensitive to one another's feelings, this shouldn't be a problem. The amount of time you *don't* spend outside your relationship could become an issue though: even two people who are simply and beautifully happy to be together will eventually get bored if they never spend time with anyone else. Surely, because you and your Cancer Guy are so sweet, you'll have plenty of friends to visit and places to go!

Leo

You and your Cancer Guy will really enjoy making one another feel good. He'll idolize and applaud you, while you sit in stunned amazement at what a great cook and caretaker he can be.

Your Cancer Guy will be forever trying to get you into bed, and not just because he is overwhelmed by your beauty. Your leadership skills and strength are the kinds of attributes he hopes to pass on to his progeny, and it's likely that he sees you as the perfect mother for his children. You'll need to discuss this with him, of course, but if and when you decide to become parents, you'll make a very well-matched pair.

Around the house, you'll want to let him do at least some of the cooking, but you'll be happier if you get to do the decorating. Add your flashy touches, and help him avoid clutter. Using your strengths to create a comfortable and happy life together will be easy, as long as you open your huge heart to embrace and accept the love of the most sensitive and caring guy you'll ever meet.

Virgo

You'll love being with your Cancer Guy, because he's caring and conscientious, just like you. He'll remember all your birthdays and anniversaries, and his sentimental gestures will make you feel valued and admired. He'll love you for always being there to take care of the little details he might have forgotten.

In bed, he may not be too precise with his technique, but he'll definitely warm your heart with his efforts to make you tingle from head to toe. Your Cancer Guy is also always thinking about what kind of baby the two of you would make together, so unless your ready for parenthood, be mindful of your protection strategies!

Around the house, Cancer can be a big help in the kitchen, but he needs guidance when it comes to housekeeping. Because he could be the reason they invented the word "Hoarder," you'll probably need to convince him to relegate some of his precious childhood mementoes to an off-site storage unit. He cherishes many things, but nothing more than the wonderful relationship he has with you, his Virgo queen.

Libra

You and your Cancer Guy will get along wonderfully well. You see him as an authority on many things, especially taking care of a household. He views you, meanwhile, as the person he wants to come home to and create a nest with.

In bed, his sensitivity and caring nature will give you great pleasure. He doesn't talk about sex as much as you do, because he considers it such a sacred act. The potential of creating new life—his baby, no less— is never far from his mind.

Around the house, you'll be the one to take care of the decorating. He has your basic grandmother's taste in furniture and will try to fill the place with antiques and bric-a-brac clutter. When it comes to culinary skills though, this guy has them in spades! Let him cook for you or take you out to eat as much as he likes. The more you can look into his deep soulful eyes, the more convinced you'll be of his Prince Charming Potential!

Scorpio

Because both you and your Cancer Guy are so intensely emotional, you don't need to do a lot of talking. His instincts are just about as sharp as yours, although he doesn't have the same strength and courage you do. He is, though, very loyal and reliable. When everyone around you has let you down, your Cancer Guy will be there, loving you just like always.

You won't be disappointed in the bedroom, either. Your Cancer Guy is fully capable of meeting you in that boundary-less world where your deepest, most transformative feelings of sexual bliss make the rest of life completely irrelevant. He'll strive to make you more emotionally aware during sex, too.

Around the house, Cancer might not always be as neat as you like, but he'll take care of other domestic chores you'd rather not be bothered with. His penchant for caretaking will be especially attractive, especially because he's always doing wonderful things to take care of *you*!

Sagittarius

You and your Cancer Guy might need to do some work before you fully understand one another, but once you do, your relationship will be more than well worth the effort! His sensitivity and clinginess can put you off at first, and he'll seem almost afraid of your frankness and honesty at times. Still, the two of you see one another as being utterly adorable.

In bed, you'll be astounded at how soon and how well Cancer gets to know your body and everything that makes you feel good. Your Cancer Guy will make you feel so comfortable that you won't even worry about making a commitment. You know he'll always be there, and yet he'll let you have enough freedom to explore things he's not really into.

Your home will be an interesting place, especially after you let your Cancer Guy take over. His nesting skills will amaze you, as he builds a physical and emotional refuge you both can run to when you want to be safe and warm.

Capricorn

You'll happily succumb to a life of bliss with your Cancer Guy, because the experience of being with your "opposite" sign will be rewarding and fulfilling. You'll love the way he can be soft, yet manly at the same time, and he'll admire your ability to go out into the world and impose your will for the greater good of the two of you and your household.

Sexually, you'll liberate Cancer from his conventional ideas about intercourse. Although he enjoys being with you physically, his mind is more on reproduction than earthly delights. He'll appreciate the way you change all that for him!

At home, the roles you play might be somewhat reversed, but you'll appreciate his nesting skills, while he looks to you for financial expertise. Whatever one of you lacks, the other will provide. You'll have to conclude, after mating with your Cancer Guy, that you truly were made for each other!

Aquarius

Keeping your Cancer Guy will mean you both have to work at understanding each other. You may struggle to understand his emotional reaction to life, and he must steel himself to accept your more detached reaction to people and events.

One of the best ways to focus more on what you share is to be good to one another in bed. Understanding his emotions gets worlds easier when you're resting in his strong and nurturing arms. Being with your Cancer Guy can feel like a trip back into a world where you find it hard to tell where your deepest primal desires end and your smart and rational mind begins.

Around the house, you'll be the one in charge of routines and schedules, while he adds those little touches that make your house a home. He'll frame photos of the two of you together and put them everywhere.

These little reminders of how happy you are with your Cancer Guy will keep the love flowing, even if they create a little clutter. Just like him, they'll grow on you!

Pisces

You and your Cancer Guy will immerse yourselves in a sea of emotions from happiness to joy, and bliss to deep, unending love. You will adore being taken in under his nurturing wing, and he'll be amazed at the cuteness with which you display genuine innocence and wonder.

In bed, you give yourselves to one another at the soul level, connecting in ways you may never have experienced with other partners. Being this close has its benefits, but it can also be scary. Be assured your Cancer Guy won't go away unless you ask him to. He's as intensely loyal as he is attentive to your needs.

Around the house, he'll be the one who makes sure you have nurturing meals and keep your traditions, while you add the artistic touches he'll admire so greatly. Your friends will all want to come and visit you because you and your Cancer Guy will build a home together based on true love!

YOUR CANCER GUY AND . . .

You might be sure you love your Cancer Guy, but how will your friends and family like him? Read on to see how he'll endear himself to all and sundry, and find out more about what kind of father and provider he might be!

Your Female Friends

The Cancer Guy will be glad you have your female friends to support you, but while you're away, he'll wonder about what you're talking about. Him, maybe? Come home with detailed stories about the conversations, right down to the shoes your bestie bought last week. Eventually, he'll get sick of hearing it and won't want to know every last detail anymore. Then you can bring the girls by the next time he makes his famous chocolate chunk cheesecake.

Your Male Friends

The Cancer Guy will probably not be too accepting of your male friends, but he won't say much about it. He'll act as though he doesn't care, but if you love him, keep him around while you visit with your guy pals. As long as he knows he's in the picture, you won't have to waste a few days begging him and his wounded ego to come back out of that desolate crab shell!

His Female Friends

You're just going to have to let the Cancer Guy have his female friends! He is so loyal and loving toward you, there's no reason to worry that he'll stray. He needs some time with other girls merely to discharge some of his nesting instincts. He'll let you come along, but you'll have to ask yourself if you're all that much into recipe swapping and the best fabrics for window coverings.

His Male Friends

The Cancer Guy will probably have some friends from school that he still clings to. It's unlikely that they're the kind of people to do anything crazy, so don't worry about him. The most you'll suffer from is his occasional upset from having too much to drink, or his feelings being hurt because the guys didn't call him when he hoped they would.

Your Family

To the Cancer Guy, family is the most important aspect of the human condition. He will respect your relatives, probably bring them gifts, and listen to all their problems. Before he's done getting to know them, you might wonder when they'll notice you're there, too! He'll do whatever it takes to fit in with your relatives, so make sure you're comfortable with that.

His Family

Even if his family members are not the best people, he'll love them anyway. Home and his family are totally sacred to the Cancer Guy. He'll run when they call and do the things they ask of him, at least most of the time. Look at it this way: if you get to the point of having your own family, he'll be even more attentive to you and your brood!

Your Pets

The Cancer Guy will take one look at your furry treasure and say "Aww!" Even if it's not furry—say a goldfish or a snake—he's still going to want to do nice things to make it feel wanted and loved. He'll also have a tendency to step in and tell you how to be a better pet handler, whether you like it or not.

His Pets

There is always an extra something kept tucked away in Cancer's household, all ready for him to take care of. You'll have to love his pets because—just like his relatives and friends—they are a part of him. The Cancer Guy won't always pick the fanciest or the most prestigious animal to be his pet, but he'll love it with all his heart until it feels that special.

His Potential for Success

The Cancer Guy will have a good career outlook, but he's never going to be a workaholic. That would mean he'd have to sacrifice too much time with you, at home, and with the rest of his family. He worries about money a lot, so he'll always find a way to put food on the table. When it comes to all the bells and whistles of a cushy material life, you might have to help out.

His Role as a Father

Always there to wipe a tear or clean up after a skinned knee, the Cancer Guy is a warm and tender father,. This is great for younger children, but when they grow, you may watch the Cancer Dad struggle to find "tough love" inside him. It will be hard for him to come down on the kids when they're in trouble, but in the end he will because he knows that's what's best for everyone.

CANCER COMPATIBILITY

Your Sign	Compatibility Level
Aries	♈♈♈♈
Taurus	♉♉♉♉
Gemini	♊♊
Cancer	♋♋♋♋
Leo	♌♌
Virgo	♍♍♍
Libra	♎♎♎
Scorpio	♏♏♏♏
Sagittarius	♐♐
Capricorn	♑♑♑♑♑
Aquarius	♒
Pisces	♓♓♓

CANCER SHORT-TERM PROSPECTS

Your Sign	Short-Term Prospects
Aries	♈♈♈♈
Taurus	♉♉♉♉
Gemini	♊♊♊
Cancer	♋
Leo	♌♌
Virgo	♍
Libra	♎♎
Scorpio	♏♏♏
Sagittarius	♐♐
Capricorn	♑♑♑
Aquarius	♒
Pisces	♓♓♓

CANCER LONG-TERM PROSPECTS

Your Sign	Long-Term Prospects
Aries	♈♈♈♈
Taurus	♉♉♉
Gemini	♊
Cancer	♋♋♋♋
Leo	♌♌
Virgo	♍♍♍
Libra	♎♎♎♎
Scorpio	♏♏♏♏
Sagittarius	♐♐
Capricorn	♑♑♑♑♑
Aquarius	♒
Pisces	♓♓♓

CHAPTER 5

Leo (July 22–August 22)

YOUR MISSION: Stroke His Ego

Leo Potential Pluses

- Strong
- Gregarious
- Funny
- Flashy
- Courageous
- Encouraging
- Charismatic
- Ambitious
- Protective
- Stylish

Leo Potential Minuses

- Bodacious
- Egotistical
- Diva-ish
- Dramatic
- Domineering
- Dismissive
- Stuck in his ways
- Self-centered
- Self-serving
- Power-hungry

WHAT THE LEO GUY HAS TO GIVE . . .

The proud, bold, and gorgeous Leo Guy has a profound effect on everybody he meets. His symbol the Lion is King of the Jungle, and one of the first things you'll notice about him is his regal manner. He seems to "own" his realm, whether it's a roomful of people or a huge audience before which he is about to speak or perform. Leo's ability to reach out to others comes from his desire to offer fatherly advice to them. He sees the potential in every person he knows and wants to help foster their talents.

It's good to know this because most people think Leo is just a pure egomaniac. It's true that he has a super-sized opinion of himself, but inside he's exceptionally tender and sweet. In his quiet moments, he realizes he needs someone to appreciate him and bring out the best of his talents too. He'll be eternally grateful if you choose to do this, and the rewards he'll give you are many.

As a Date:

Leo won't ask you to go out with him: he'll inform you that you're going out on a date with him. His confidence can be very attractive, so unless you have an irreversible aversion to guys with strong egos, you'll probably go wherever he suggests. Most likely, your first dates will involve a mixture of conversation and lively activities. Dancing, clubbing, ball games, and cultural events are all activities Leo enjoys and will want to share with you. He'll want to test your ability to enjoy things the way he does, and if you pass muster, he'll call you again and right away. His ruling planet the Sun pumps him full of enthusiasm. Once he decides he likes you, he'll want to see you as often and as much as possible.

As a Sex Partner:

If you like to be swept off your feet and carried into the lion's den to be loved, cherished, and thrilled by a man's utter sexual prowess, you're going to love the Leo Guy. He's strong and sensual, yet he can be as tender as he is ardent when it comes to making love. He's not pushy, but he doesn't leave you wondering if he's interested.

Once in bed, there won't be much of a choice but to allow him to lead the proceedings. He'll talk to you and tell you how beautiful you are because he wants you to feel a moment of conquest. His orgasms are just like him, explosive and showy. He'll be very intent, though, on bringing you to a climax first. His moment of culmination wouldn't be complete unless he knew he succeeded in making you feel totally, absolutely fabulous.

As a Life Partner:

The Leo Guy is definitely the kind to couple up and create a household with you. He wants to be your protector, and he also looks forward to having children to lead and cultivate. Around home, he'll expect to be treated as king, but you can still get him to pitch in with housework. He'll be especially adept at polishing windows and mirrors . . . why? He loves to look at his reflection! (He's also particularly fond of his hair and will always go that extra mile to keep it looking its best.)

From you, all he wants is to be proud of what you are like and what your home looks like. He'll enjoy entertaining, and when he brings people back to his dashing den, he'll want it to make a fabulous impression. The color orange and brassy fixtures will be a few of the things he favors, along with bar equipment so he can mix drinks for friends.

Emotionally:

The Leo Guy can be very emotional, but he won't always let you see what he's feeling, unless it's upbeat and positive. A born leader, he wants to inspire you and everyone he knows to do their best. So, even when he feels like giving up, he won't let you know it. Once you get to know him, though, you'll be able to tell when he's unhappy. That's when you'll step in and do what you have to in order to bring him back to his old self. Start by telling him how fantastic he is and why you love him so much. Point out how he's helped other people and how much of a difference he's made in their lives. Before long, you'll see his head rise and his chest push out, and before you know it, he'll *roar* . . . and then drag you off to the bedroom. Success!

FIND YOUR LEO GUY!

The Leo Guy isn't hard to pick out of a crowd. His booming voice, the proud way he holds up his head, and the zest for life he displays are just some of the things you'll notice right away. He'll realize you see him: he's ultrasensitive to the people he draws in as he builds an audience around him. Catch his eye by focusing all your attention on him, and he'll probably start talking.

He'll pay lots of attention to the way you dress and whether your attire is appropriate to what you're doing. Don't show up for clubbing wearing jeans, and leave the strappy sandals home when he suggests a picnic in the park or a long walk along the beach. It's also important for you to be cool and confident. Above all, what he's looking for is a woman who is as strong, confident, and savvy as he is!

The Leo Guy is popular, so you're going to have to play to his personality if you want to stand out from the crowd. Read on to see how you can use the traits of your sign to connect with Leo in a way that really clicks.

Aries

The Leo Guy is going to notice you right away, so be ready for him! He'll sense your fiery spirit and know instinctively that the two of you will be fast friends. You'll instantly take a liking to him, too. Here's a guy who's every bit as strong and energetic as you are and isn't afraid to let you know he's into you. He'll love your zest for life and figure the two of you can be up all night long, painting the town your favorite colors: red and gold!

Your outbursts of temper won't frighten him, and as long as you don't hurt anyone, he'll let you vent. Still, he'll try hard to cultivate patience in you. That's something he's probably come to learn and embrace as a very useful ally of an attribute in his life. Try not to nix his recommendations, even if you go to the same places all the time. Apply friendly nudges to introduce him to the delights of variety, and he'll thank you a million times over!

Taurus

Although you're nowhere near as much of a showy sort as the Leo Guy is, you share the same desire to keep your environment predictable while enjoying a variety of sensual pleasures, too. While he might enjoy going places where the atmosphere is lavish, you'll pick a spot because of the quality of the food and the people who work there. You'll both love being pampered and cared for, and will go out of your way to make each other happy.

Sometimes, though, he'll have problems understanding why you get so nervous. He'll tell you that everything is going to work out, because he has a blind faith in his ability to make that so. You'll have to learn to live with this, especially when things don't work out the way he planned.

With all his faults, the Leo Guy is still a great match for you. He'll inspire you to be more daring and courageous, while you show him practical ways to make his ideas more profitable.

Gemini

The Leo Guy might be hard for you to understand, especially at first. You have a hard time comprehending how a person can be blatantly egoistic, because you live in a world where everyone is on equal footing. Still, there's a lot you like about Leo. He's strong, entertaining, and dynamic. Conversations with him never fail to have a lot of spark, and you enjoy sharing all your news with him.

The Leo Guy likes your independence and admires your mental and verbal skills. He'll test them from time to time, because although he might be more physically and socially active than mentally, he'll probably have impeccable grammar. He'll encourage you, especially if you're one of those people who has always wanted to write a novel or produce a song and hasn't yet done it. Leo takes it on as his job to ensure you live up to your full potential and finish what you start. You'll feel stronger just having him there to cheer you on.

Cancer

The Leo Guy is adorable and strong, but there's something about him that puts you off a little. While you enjoy being motherly and want to coddle the man you love, he will push you to do things that get you ahead in the world. He'll admire the way you take care of him and want to take care of others, but he would prefer it if you balanced your life with a bit of taking care of yourself.

Although you'll admire his strength and courage, his self-centeredness could get on your nerves at times. You'll want to promote the idea of him taking more time to deal with the needs of other people, starting with you! Going out with the Leo Guy can seem like a ride on a see-saw, but if you can reach a point of equilibrium, chances are the two of you will benefit greatly from trying to bend toward one another and enjoying a strong, solid friendship.

Leo

You know you're a tough customer and demand a lot from the people you keep close in your circle of friends and family. That's why going out with another Leo can easily become a challenge. Yet, there will be something so magnetic about meeting a man who seems to be your "other half." In the end, you won't be able to resist the Leo Guy. He'll love your courage and admire your looks. He'll see you as the kind of "top shelf" date he is proud to have on his arm.

You'll like being treated like a lady when he's with you, including the part where he feels he has chosen you above all others. It's hard to find another guy who appreciates where you're coming from on issues such as your desire to be admired, so why look any further? You might have some battles over who's in the spotlight at any given time, but with some work, you'll learn how to take turns, and share that warm glow.

Virgo

You'll smile to yourself when you first see the Leo Guy. His strong, dynamic personality will attract you, but you'll also be wary of his bravado. Why would someone who's really all that confident need such a great deal of attention?

The Leo Guy is truly someone different underneath all that ego and self-centered pretense. Remember, he truly wants to see everyone develop their best qualities and talents, and he uses his leadership skills to draw the people he wants to help toward him. He'll love your sharp wit and appreciate your somewhat cynical sense of humor. He'll keep working on getting your attention until he grows on you. Although you may constantly need proof he's telling the truth, there's a lot of fun to be had with a Leo Guy!

He'll take you to clubs, shows, and events you might never get to alone or with other men, and once he decides he desires and adores you, he'll treat you like his queen!

Libra

You and the Leo Guy will have a lot in common, but those things can cause a few little problems. Both of you will want to get plenty of attention for the way you look, for one. You're both beautiful in different ways, and together you'll make one very handsome couple!

He'll love the way you put together your look and be very proud to take you out to show his friends how well he's done. You'll be smug about being with him as well, because he's strong, dynamic, and courageous. Your friends will be happy for you, if just a touch jealous.

You'll need to work on supporting each other rather than trying to compete to see who's better looking or who's getting the most attention. When you spend your time trying to please one another, you'll build a bridge that brings you close together, and you'll both feel great about that.

Scorpio

You'll see how you and the Leo Guy make a great match almost from the moment you meet. His flash and panache make a stark contrast to your quiet and more reserved approach, but you admire his ability to seek excellence and stand out from the crowd. He'll love your ability to go into depth in order to get to the facts and figures you need to be the best at what you do.

The other thing Leo will love about you is your lack of fascination for the spotlight. While you like to be sequestered away on the sidelines, he relishes being out there front and center for everyone to see. Don't worry, though: his ego isn't really as huge as it seems. In truth, when you're alone with him, you'll find that the big, bad lion is more like a little lamb. Tell him how magnificent he is, and he'll be yours forever. That means, when this kingly man takes you on, you get to be royalty, too.

Sagittarius

Hanging out with the Leo Guy is like being with your very best friend. From the moment you meet him, you'll feel a kinship that's pretty rare. Although your form of fire is more refined, you find his raw energy very attractive. Where you're boisterous and adventurous, he's bold and courageous. You'll love the way he always seems so confident and in control of his destiny.

He might not be as physically active as you are, but he makes up for it with his ability to inspire people. He'll be excited to show you new things, and bring out your best qualities even more than you do on your own.

You'll impress him with your knowledge and ability to be completely spontaneous. Although he won't be as wild about spur-of-the-moment activities as you are, he'll love being dragged away on occasional wild escapades. The two of you will have plenty of fun, lots to talk about, and many, many nights of sizzling passion.

Capricorn

The showy Leo Guy might not seem to be your type when you first meet him, but when you study his approach to the world, you'll eventually see his seemingly huge ego is only a mask he wears to bring people into his circle.

When you're alone with him, the Leo Guy will show you a softer side that's sweet and sexy. He'll be in awe of your expertise in so many different areas, and he'll wish he could be as truly confident as you are. Boost his ego by pointing out the reasons why he can easily command at least as much authority as you, and don't compete with him. When he sees you're willing to love him just as he is, he'll get more comfortable and display less bossy, domineering behavior.

The two of you might not be crazy about one another at first, but once you discover and develop a healthy mutual respect, you'll both decide to keep on trying, no matter what.

Aquarius

You'll be so happy to meet a Leo Guy! At last, you will have discovered a man who's capable of keeping up with your (high speed) train of thought, and is strong and dynamic enough to realize you don't have to be on top of each other every waking minute. He'll love your independent thinking and only encourage you to continue to discover your own ideas and help spread them as far and wide as you can.

While you're cool and detached, the Leo Guy is overheated and passionate. When you get together, you'll calm him down and he'll bring you to life. You might never have known you could be as happy as you are when you're with this human dynamo. He'll love showing you off to his friends and bragging about your clear and potent intellect. He can get dramatic from time to time, and when that annoys you, it's okay to tell him. He'll do everything he can to please you because he knows you're the only one who can really make him purr.

Pisces

Don't be afraid of the Leo Guy. Although he might roar like a lion while he's in public, in private he's just a little pussycat. His commanding presence always attracts a crowd, but don't worry: with your gentle beauty and intense attention, he'll definitely notice you.

He'll deeply admire your creativity and imagination. In some cases, you can find the Leo Guy to be a great collaborator. You dream up the story, and he acts it out! This can be a whole lot of fun in your sex life, to be sure, and it can also translate into ideas that open up business options.

You'll love the way he instinctively knows how to bring out the best in you and doesn't give up, even when you seem to be hopelessly off-track. It can take some work for the two of you to meet in the middle, but once you do, you'll both be happier than you've been in a very long while.

KEEP YOUR LEO GUY!

After your Leo Guy decides he can't live without you, how can you keep him thinking that way? Don't count on his need for predict-ability to keep him interested in everything you do: when it comes to love, Leo needs constant stimulation and more attention than you thought possible! You have to make sure that, at least once or twice a day, you do and say some things that will stroke his ego.

Compliment his clothing, and he'll shake that gorgeous mane of hair. Add that his hair looks fabulous, and his chest will stick out. Then, when you ask when you can make love again because he knows how to take your breath away, he just might roar with pride! Once you get this routine down in several variations, you'll be on the road to maintaining your relationship and keeping him happy and generous . . . just the way you love him!

Keeping your Leo Guy will take some fast thinking and a lot of what he has—confidence and courage. Read on to see how you can best prove to your Leo Guy that you're the one who's willing to rise to his challenges, and treat him like the royalty he firmly believes he is.

Aries

You and your Leo Guy will keep one another hopping! Make sure you keep tabs on each other's individual schedules, though. If you don't, you could become overbooked and disappointed when you have to go solo to an event that's much more fun when you go as a couple.

Sexually, the two of you will create a hotbed of passion. One of you is more passionate than the other, and fortunately, you take turns! You might have to re-invent your approach now and then, but your Leo Guy will be amenable to you being the one to seduce him. He'll love it when you abandon your sporty clothes for a very girly negligee! When he gets things started, you'll be totally turned on by the way he sweeps in there and carries you away.

Around the house, you'll have to prod him some to get to household chores, but eventually he'll take responsibility. He'll become more flexible when you get to be more persistent.

Taurus

The strong draw between you and your Leo Guy has to do with your mutual desire to have a passionate, yet predictable love affair. He'll love and support you and try to allay your fears. All you need to do is remember to tell him how great he looks and how good he is to you, and he'll stick to you like glue.

In bed, he'll provide all those things you want, from shoulder rubs and soft kisses to deep, passionate moments that make you scream . . . in a good way! He'll love the way you adore him, as you coo in ecstasy and set out to please him with at least as much pleasure as he gave you.

Housework won't be his forte, but he's great at supervising cleaners and contractors. While there will be times when you wish he was not so high maintenance, your Leo Guy will bring a lot of great things to your life. Open your heart and let him in.

Gemini

You and your Leo Guy will have to work at the art of sticking together, because you both have strong drives to go out and meet new people. You need a lot more freedom than he does, but he still will want to have moments where he's the only one people are looking at or listening to.

In bed, do what you can to reassure him that you are his alone, mainly by using every last technique you know to bring him to one of his dramatic, explosive orgasms. He'll reciprocate by finding all those spots on your back and arms that make you tingle until you blow up in a sea of sensation and colors in the backs of your eyes.

Your Leo Guy's temper and list of demands can be two things that turn you off, but if you keep the focus on how much you turn each other on, there will be no trouble in paradise.

Cancer

You and your Leo Guy might have a lot of passion between you, but if you want to stick together, you're going to have to work at it. While your sign is ruled by the changeable Moon, his is ruled by the strong and energetic Sun. There will be times when he wants to drag you to active events and places that will stretch your stamina, and he won't love staying home the way you do.

Try to get him to see why being alone in the bedroom is worth cutting himself off from the rest of the world for a little while. No one can take care of a lover the way you do, not when you can anticipate every need and make your Leo Guy feel as though you live for the sole purpose of loving him.

While he might not be so sensitive, he's definitely strong and protective. The adventure of being all you can be is the reward for sticking with your Leo Guy.

Leo

Certainly you admire your own personality enough to know there could never be anyone quite as dashing and attractive as your Leo Guy. The two of you have great potential for sticking together, but first you have to get down with the idea of sharing the spotlight. This will require a careful balance of yielding to his desires and talking about what you need. Things will work out best if you both remember that being assertive is fine, until it develops into an aggressive game of "Who's the Boss?"

Take turns playing "predator and prey" in the bedroom. He'll like chasing you down almost more than he adores having you grab him, kiss him with all your womanly strength, and smother him in your rapture. Most likely, he'll reciprocate by ensuring you both explode in a fiery blast of mutual admiration. Let him lead when you go out socially, and you'll discover the joys of having doors opened and your seat pulled out from the table for you at luxe restaurants and posh dinner parties.

Virgo

Your Leo Guy is adorable, and you know he admires you, because everywhere you go he's always bragging about how glad he is to have found you. You have a knack for solving life's little problems for him, and he truly does appreciate it. In turn, he helps you get through situations that require more of a backbone than you prefer to exert.

In bed, both of you have a lot of fun. He enjoys watching you succumb with abandon to his passionate advances, while you dig turning him on in a different way every time you have sex.

Around the house, you'll be the one in charge of keeping things neat. He'll keep more of an eye on long-term projects that require his way of providing leadership and strategy. Life with your Leo Guy will never be simple, but it'll add so much excitement to your life, you'll want it to go on and on forever.

Libra

Your Leo Guy is a superstar, like you, but you each have different songs to sing. His is loud and boisterous, while yours would be soft and mesmerizing. The two of you make a spectacular appearance as a couple, and people's heads will turn as soon as you enter the room.

In bed, he'll be very demonstrative, which is always a turn-on for you. He'll love the way you admire him, gently stroke him, and massage his ego by giving him nonverbal signals of your undying love.

Around the house, Leo won't be the first one to volunteer to cook or clean, but he'll definitely have strong opinions about your joint decorating style. Let him pick out the fixtures in the kitchen and bathroom. He has impeccable taste, just like you! While you and Leo are a little bit different, there are a lot of things you do together that make all the work it takes to get along well worth it.

Scorpio

Life with your Leo Guy will stimulate you intellectually and sexually. His irresistible good looks and fiery potency will absorb your sexual attention while his way of offering leadership will intrigue you.

Your Leo Guy will never fail to provide you with enough sexual inspiration to satisfy you. All he has to do is show up, and you will melt. In turn, your deeply emotional and spiritual way of sharing your body permits him to see into your soul.

Around the house, you'll get along well because you both like to finish what you start. When it comes to cleaning the house or cooking, he'll be more eager to do it for you than for anyone else, because to him, you represent "home." While you might imagine life with someone as strong-willed as you would be a chore, it can be sheer bliss when you get together with your Leo Guy.

Sagittarius

You and your Leo Guy will watch your relationship take off like a rocket! He'll adore your way of setting out for spontaneous adventures, while you'll love his way of teaching you how to take your experiences and make them work for you. Even though you're sharp and intelligent, your Leo Guy is street smart. He'll be determined to bring the best out in you, and teach you common sense ways of capitalizing on your skills.

In bed, your Leo Guy will test your abilities to the max. The two of you will have a lot of passion, and you'll have to stick around to show it to him again and again. Although his strong-willed exterior might make you think otherwise, that super-sized ego of his is as fake as a cheap toupee. He is very tender on the inside, and will need you to tell him how great he is, whether you're having sex or getting ready to brush your teeth in the morning.

He's not the best at housekeeping because his royal manner would much rather supervise "the help." You'll find a way to get all the cooking and cleaning done, while the two of you indulge yourselves in your magical, wonderful relationship.

Capricorn

You and your Leo Guy have a bit of work to do, but there are ways to make your relationship seem easy. His flashy manner doesn't always go down so well with you, but the minute you begin to see it for what it is—a façade he uses to summon up his courage—your attitude will change.

Show your love for your Leo Guy in bed, and he'll instantly fuel up on the attention you're providing. He needs to know you love him now and always. Once he's confident of that, he'll stop acting all silly and dramatic.

Around the house, he won't be excited about getting his royal hands dirty, but if he'll listen to anyone, it would be you. Because your sign is ruled by Saturn and his is ruled by the Sun, he looks to you to contain him and structure his activities. You won't mind doing this, because life with your Leo Guy will make you feel awake and alive!

Aquarius

Your scientific mind has no trouble believing that opposites attract, so when you and your Leo Guy decide to get serious, you'll feel this same principle with your heart. While you impress him with emotional detachment and the ability to assess people, he's passionate and dramatic in a way that makes him impossible to resist.

When you get into bed, this will be even more apparent. His desire for you will seem insatiable, and the way you respond with such fervor will feed his ego while he builds up to an amazing orgasm!

Let him be the one to determine who should do which household chores and when; he'll have a knack for identifying each of your strengths. Cooking, cleaning, and caretaking will be made better by your partnership, and if you decide to have children, they couldn't have a better dad. This romantic, supportive match will provide life-long joys of being in love!

Pisces

What happens when you fall for your Leo Guy, who electrifies you from head to toe? All the rules go out the window. You and your Leo Guy will have problems seeing life in the same way. He'll want to throw away a lot of the little collections you accrue around the house, and you might be able to let go of a few. Just don't let him take away too much. When he feels like his ego isn't being massaged enough, your Leo Guy can have a tendency to become domineering.

In bed, this isn't such a problem! You'll enjoy having him take charge of your body, while you use all your creative techniques to ensure he gets everything possible from having sex with you.

Late at night, when no one else is around, your Leo Guy won't be cleaning; however, he'll be lying in wait in your bed, hoping you'll decide to join him in there as soon as humanly possible.

YOUR LEO GUY AND . . .

Now that you know how to bond better with your Leo Guy, read on to unveil some of the surprises that might arise when you get your relationship with him to mesh with the rest of your life.

Your Female Friends

Your Leo Guy is a showoff, so of course he's going to want to show what he's got in front of your female friends. There's nothing more to this than him getting the girls to tell you how lucky you are to have him. He'll enjoy being with them and being the center of attention for just a few minutes; then he'll let you go off with the girls.

Your Male Friends

You and your male friends might have an understanding about what you are to each other, but the Leo Guy won't buy it. He trusts you all right, but he knows how men think, and he'll be on his guard. He'll watch you with your guy friends closely and want to go with you just to make sure you all remember what the real deal is . . . you belong to *him*!

His Female Friends

There will always be women chasing your Leo Guy around. He's so dynamic and strong, and women love him. You'll have to keep faith in the fact that he loves you, and trust him when he says these friendships are simply platonic. Loyalty is Leo's watchword. He very rarely wavers from the one he loves.

His Male Friends

Being the alpha-male in just about any group he joins, your Leo Guy is going to have a large selection of male friends. He can't resist the captive audience! He'll want to talk with them about guy stuff, too. Some of this will include his life with you, but as long as you keep him happy, why worry? He's probably out there bragging about you.

Your Family

Your Leo Guy is respectful and respectable, and your family will love him. He might not jump in and start wearing the matching family hats at first, though. He has to find out whether he's comfortable spending a lot of time with them, and then you'll be able to tell if he's just putting up with them or if he feels the love.

His Family

The Leo Guy will always be good to his family because he is so loyal. He'll want to give them gifts and shower them with affection. Of course, he'll always look to them for a source of love, too. He'll always try to please them by doing great things that make them proud to be related to him.

Your Pets

The Leo Guy's tender side will come out when he meets your pets. This proud and noble man will become soft and cuddly as a kitty when he meets your animal friends. He'll relate especially well to felines, naturally, but he'll like dogs almost as much. He realizes your pet is important to you and will quickly try to win affection so the pet won't get jealous. He will also push to become the "dominant creature."

His Pets

If he has pets, they're very likely to be for a practical purpose. He'll have a cat for mousing or a watchdog to protect his property. He's a firm believer in giving his animals jobs, so they're probably pretty well disciplined. He will also enjoy the social aspect of pet ownership, like meeting people at the dog park.

His Potential for Success

Because pride is the driving force behind most things Leo does, he'll have the makings of a winner in the work force. He's very strong-willed, alpha-male type, so most times he'll be in a position of power or at least have a job that gives him the capability to earn more than enough to take care of himself and the people he loves.

His Role as Father

Truly, Leo is the perfect father. Although he isn't patient with children who won't try hard, he'll push them until they get the kind of motivation they need to survive in the cold, cruel world. He'll always bring out the best in his children and strike a beautiful balance between unconditional support and tough love. He'll always take charge of the situation and allow your children to feel safe and secure.

LEO COMPATIBILITY

Your Sign	Compatibility Level
Aries	♈♈♈♈
Taurus	♉♉♉
Gemini	♊♊♊
Cancer	♋♋
Leo	♌♌
Virgo	♍♍
Libra	♎♎♎
Scorpio	♏♏♏♏
Sagittarius	♐♐♐♐
Capricorn	♑♑♑
Aquarius	♒♒♒♒♒
Pisces	♓♓♓

LEO SHORT-TERM PROSPECTS

Your Sign	Short-Term Prospects
Aries	♈♈♈♈
Taurus	♉♉♉♉
Gemini	♊♊
Cancer	♋
Leo	♌♌♌
Virgo	♍
Libra	♎♎
Scorpio	♏♏♏♏
Sagittarius	♐♐♐♐
Capricorn	♑♑
Aquarius	♒♒♒
Pisces	♓

LEO LONG-TERM PROSPECTS

Your Sign	Long-Term Prospects
Aries	♈♈♈
Taurus	♉♉♉♉
Gemini	♊♊
Cancer	♋♋
Leo	♌♌♌
Virgo	♍♍
Libra	♎♎♎
Scorpio	♏♏♏♏
Sagittarius	♐♐♐♐
Capricorn	♑♑♑
Aquarius	♒♒♒♒♒
Pisces	♓

CHAPTER 6

Virgo (August 23–September 21)

YOUR MISSION: Let Him Deal with the Nitty-Gritty

Virgo Potential Pluses

- Nurturing
- Detail-oriented
- Dedicated
- Cooperative
- Discerning
- Task-oriented
- Industrious
- Determined
- Service-oriented
- Horticulturally gifted

Virgo Potential Minuses

- Critical
- Obsessive
- Overly focused
- Nit-picky
- Unimaginative
- Unadventurous
- Distant
- Detached
- Subservient
- Demanding

WHAT THE VIRGO GUY HAS TO GIVE . . .

Though his discerning and sometimes critical nature makes him seem otherwise, there's a tremendous amount of sweetness and kindness in the Virgo Guy's heart. His symbol, the Vestal Virgin, is usually pictured separating the wheat from the chaff, and this is exactly what he does. His practical nature pushes him to find what's useful in every situation he encounters and put aside the irrelevant and distracting elements.

Sometimes, while he's doing this, people think he's being critical or dismissive. This isn't the case at all. In truth, the Virgo Guy simply wants to be of service. When he gives instructions or makes suggestions, it's almost always rooted in his desire to do good deeds for others. Remember that when he tells you there's a string on your hem or lipstick on your teeth! He just doesn't want you to go around looking anything less than perfect.

He's one of the hardest workers you'll ever meet. He can't stand to be anything but busy, so don't worry about him. If he didn't have "too much" to do, he wouldn't be nearly as happy. Pamper him when he makes time in that schedule to see you, and let him do what he does best: take care of all the little details you probably forgot.

As a Date:

The Virgo Guy will show up on time and expect you to do the same. There are only so many hours in the day, and the ones he sets aside for rest and relaxation are especially important. His reputation for being "all work and no play" is exaggerated. Sure, he'll have a plan for your time together, but he has a flexible part of his nature that allows him to adapt it to fit the suggestions you make.

When you first meet, he'll be looking at you to determine how much potential you have to grow as a person and how willing you are to take his suggestions. He'll also be watching to see how capable you are of taking care of him. Although he *can* deal with life all on his own, he wants to be loved, nurtured, and fussed over, too.

As a Sex Partner:

Despite his appearance as a prim-and-proper person, the Virgo Guy can be pretty hot in bed. He's inspired to express himself this way by the urge to be close and devoted to you. At some point in his life, he's probably spent time studying up on sex and the various ways of turning you on. His mastery of technique, coupled with his genuine sense of caring, can be very effective. He'll study you and your reactions to the way he seduces and excites you, and by the time he's done, you'll feel like a really lucky woman!

He's not so horny that he never thinks of anything else, though. Sex is a part of life for him, and while it isn't the center of his universe, you'll get evidence that just as it was for his symbol, celibacy is only a transient condition. As soon as he has the time, he'll find ways to be all over you!

As a Domestic Partner:

The Virgo Guy is usually very neat, especially with his personal belongings. Some have even been known to hang their jeans in the closet, "filed" according to the degree of fading and shade. Around the rest of the house, any job that allows him to tend to details and see immediate results of his work will suit him well. He'll happily wash dishes or polish furniture.

To a Virgo Guy, everything has a place, and if it doesn't, it has to go. There are some exceptions, though. A very few Virgo Guys display the opposite kind of behavior. The quest for domestic perfection is difficult, and when these types don't achieve it, they give up totally. A rogue Virgo Guy like this can create a living space that's hazardous to the health of anyone who enters! Hope for the first type. Despite his fussiness, he's far easier to live around!

Emotionally:

The Virgo Guy is sensible and practical, but he also has some interesting emotions. He won't express them publicly, necessarily, but he'll let you know how he feels about lots of people and things, especially you. He's prone toward making romantic gestures, from sending flowers to leaving little notes to remind you of what you did the last time you were in bed.

When the Virgo Guy gets angry, he'll come across more as being irritated than enraged. He tends to control his emotions, sometimes sublimating them to the point of allowing stress to affect his body. When he complains of a stomach ache or vague intestinal symptoms, you might want to ask him what you can do to ease his worries or be a better partner to him. He'll discuss these issues rather than yell at you, but his pointed criticism can sting. Try to remember: your Virgo Guy is always trying to help you on your own quest for self-improvement.

FIND YOUR VIRGO GUY!

Love is something the average Virgo Guy will never go without for very long. He'll always be looking for the right significant other to have in his life, and if you're lucky, it'll be you! You'll have to be on your toes and able to observe and appreciate his ability to deal with the details.

Talk to him about what he's thinking, and he'll point out items and incidents you might not have considered before. Do your best to be neat and clean, and show him your appreciation if he points out in any way at all how your life can be improved. Your willingness to learn will be the number one attraction factor as far as he's concerned, so steel yourself for a bit of constructive criticism.

If you want a Virgo Guy's attention, you're going to have to be as attentive to details as he is. Use the information below to determine how to use your sign's strong points to make yourself irresistibly attractive to the Virgo Guy.

Aries

When the Virgo Guy points out a stain or some other imperfection in your appearance, there's a lot of love behind his eyes. He'll adore your strong and lively spirit and hope you'll pause your high-action pattern of movement long enough to stop and notice him.

You'll like the way he seems to have his life in control and hope that maybe he'll organize yours a little bit better, too. He's calm and collected, at least on the outside, but he can get nervous and edgy. When this happens, and he snaps at you, don't be offended. He's as impatient as you are, but in a different way. He has a hard time understanding why you can't see life as a process that must be left to unfold. Waiting for him to come around and stake his claim on you could be excruciating, but it won't kill you. It'll be worth it to wait to get close to the kind, gentle, and helpful Virgo Guy.

Taurus

You and the Virgo Guy share a point of view that puts practicality first. You'll point out issues that seem unrealistic to each other and tend to worry about the same things. Money is important to both of you, because you share a desire to be at least comfortable.

He might have a different definition of what's essential to your happiness, though. Your Virgo Guy really does live by the old adage, "waste not, want not," and he would rather not have to "want" for anything!

He's far more flexible than you in other ways, though, especially when it comes to making plans with people. Though both of you are prone to managing the details of any event you decide to organize or attend, you tend to panic when things go awry, while he'll be there ready to offer spur-of-the-moment solutions. Life could get a lot less stressful for you with the Virgo Guy around to show you the art of rolling with the punches.

Gemini

The attraction of the Virgo Guy will call to you from across the room. Here's someone who seems to have his act together, yet is also curious enough to listen to what you have to say. He's also very good-looking and has enough of an air of mystery about him to get your curiosity going.

He'll love your ability to blast through the walls of shyness and get right to the conversation with just about everyone you meet. He'll enjoy meeting your friends, too. In fact, he may pay far too much attention to keeping tabs on you than you'd like! Don't worry. He fully intends on allowing you enough rope to go out and continue to collect networking and business contacts. When it comes to flirting with other men, though, he might use a lasso to pull you in. Once he gets you in his arms and you become his little project, he won't want to lose you!

Cancer

From the first time you meet the Virgo Guy, and he wipes your chin or helps you pick up the pen you dropped, you'll be amazed that for once, someone is taking care of you! You won't be bothered much by Virgo's efforts to make you into a more perfect person. You understand his vision of the world, and even when you don't quite measure up to it, you realize he's only trying to get everyone he knows to try a little harder.

He'll adore the way you cater to his needs and will feel very much the same way you do about meeting someone who really seems to care. You'll easily agree on where to go on your dates and will often opt for the quiet nights at home that you crave. A big bonus will be the Virgo Guy's liking for the kitchen, particularly his enthusiasm for cleaning up after one of your grand cooking extravaganzas!

Leo

You and the Virgo Guy will be very attracted to one another because you sense that each has something the other could use to bring both of you into better balance. Focused, organized, and discerning, the Virgo Guy has class and finesse. He's also a great listener. He'll be enamored by your flash and courage, and able to help you organize your activities so you always know where you're supposed to be, and when.

The Virgo Guy will appreciate your confident demeanor, but he'll see right through you when you display a false sense of ego. This can be a relief or it can be crushing, depending on how far you've gone toward admitting you're not always as much in charge in things as you pretend. The Virgo Guy will see what really goes on behind your "throne," and yet he'll love you even when you're not on the top of the world. Knowing you have your Virgo Guy there to help pick you up can be a very warm and comforting experience.

Virgo

Meeting a fellow Virgo will be a wonderful moment for you. You'll find one another right away, maybe at a reception, scrutinizing the canapés and discerning which ingredients are needed to make them far more palatable. When your eyes meet, you'll burst into laughter, because more than anyone, you notice how your penchant for perfection takes you to extremes at times.

He'll love the way you take care of things for him and always remember how you like your favorite food and drinks. You'll adore the fact that you don't have to remind him of the dates you make, because his memory is just as good as yours. In fact, he'll join you in selecting activities for the two of you to enjoy together.

As long as the two of you can avoid competing to see who's neater, more efficient, and more organized, you can be exceptionally contented, as you nurture one another along the road to happiness.

Libra

You'll love meeting a Virgo Guy. He'll ask you where you bought your clothes and how you put your look together. His own sleek, neat appearance will appeal to you, and you'll admire the way he doesn't hesitate to tell people when they can do something better. He'll be acutely aware of your ability to see both sides of a situation and respect you for not being overly judgmental.

One area that could cause you difficulty is decision-making. He makes choices based on facts and figures, as do you . . . well that and instincts, intuition, the weather, the ambient temperature, and popular opinion. He tends to make up his mind a lot faster than you, and if you want to catch this high-value guy while you can, you'd better speed up your process before he gives up and goes in another direction. If you get him to stay, you'll feel like a very lucky person to have this handsome, well-organized, and focused guy doing everything he can to make you smile.

Scorpio

You'll enjoy meeting the Virgo Guy. You'll use your instincts to discern that both of you are after the same thing: perfection! You have a deep understanding of the big picture of your "perfect" world, and he's totally capable of working out the details.

You'll love his businesslike manner and his adaptability. You can work out things to do and places to go through a process of mutual agreement that only improves every plan you make. He'll love you for your ability to persist despite all the obstacles and also for your unmistakable sexuality.

The only thing that might get in your way is a tendency for you to be too manipulative. When you lose your ability to engage in give-and-take, your relationship with the Virgo Guy won't work as well. Instead of being upset when he doesn't fall for your ploys to gain complete control, you can appreciate you've found someone who's as smart and perceptive as you are. That will let your Virgo Guy know how much you respect him and help you build the kind of relationship you've been after all along.

Sagittarius

When you first meet the Virgo Guy, there will be lots of sparks. Both of you are adaptable and open to suggestions from others, and as you get to know the Virgo Guy, you'll find he has more than a few!

He loves your sense of wonder and your ability to carry on several adventures at once, and you admire how he organizes his life, in ways you've only read about in the self-help books you may keep in your library.

He may not be terribly tolerant of your wild streak, though, especially the part of it that inspires you to strew your clothing and belongings all over the place. Even before he comes into your home, he'll probably speak to you about the importance of neatness. If you can get past his nit-picking, and he can learn to accept your household abandon, the two of you can live a life that brings both of you out of your usual ruts and into a world of passion and love.

Capricorn

You and the Virgo Guy will have an easy time getting along because you both have an earthy, grounded approach to life. Since you're such a big-picture person, you'll probably be grateful for his discerning eye for detail. Also, you're not so sensitive as to take all the criticisms he makes too personally.

He might resist your attempts to get him to look at the big picture, but if you appeal to his logic, he'll have to see the sense in letting you do the long-term planning.

You see the big picture while Virgo sees the need to take care of details, so find a way to work together that lets you benefit from the best of both perspectives. Don't be afraid to be the one in charge of starting up the passion, though. Because you're such cozy, good friends, your Virgo Guy could forget all about the incredible fun the two of you can have—but you'll never let that happen!

Aquarius

You and the Virgo Guy have an interesting vibe together. You both have a similar vision, in that you'd like to see the world be made better in some way, yet, you have entirely different ways of doing it.

You'll love the way he spells things out with as little emotion as possible, as well as how he thinks things through with pure rational skill. He'll adore your ideas, and the way you exercise your personal freedom. Even though he's happy the way he is, there will be some part of him that wishes he could be as much of a visionary as you are.

There might be times when you wish he would stop talking before he bursts your bubble, but for the most part you'll be able to overlook his tendency to poke holes in your plans because they aren't practical. After all, you can't help being fascinated by the articulate, smart, and compassionate Virgo Guy.

Pisces

You'll fall head over heels for the Virgo Guy the minute you see him! He seems to answer all the questions you have about life, from "how do I manage my finances?" to "what should I wear to my next job interview?" His soft, compassionate way of talking to you will be soothing and encouraging.

He'll love you for your ability to be creative and courageous in your own way. He gets timid about breaking convention and wishes he could dream with sweet abandon the way you do. You'll admire the way he tends to you and shares the kind of compassion you feel for all of humanity. For the most part, his caring is directed more toward individuals, and one of them will definitely be you!

You and the Virgo Guy are a strong, "opposites attract" kind of match. With even the smallest bit of effort, the two of you will have a very long and happy life of togetherness.

KEEP YOUR VIRGO GUY!

He's practical, helpful, and skilled in everything from making home improvements to making love. All your friends tell you it must be wonderful to have a guy like him around all the time. So, now that you've found your wonderful, helpful, and loving Virgo Guy, what can you do to make sure he stays by your side? You'll have to respond to all those not-so-gentle suggestions of his. He'll keep looking out for you, but at some point you're going to have to show him you're making your own attempts to be a better person.

He'll also need you to take care of him from time to time. All the worries he has from work and his other responsibilities can become overwhelming. Nothing will calm him down like a warm, heartfelt hug and a healthy meal. Do these things for your Virgo Guy, and he'll be good to you for as long as you want!

Read on to see how you can use the qualities of your sign to appeal to the Virgo Guy as much as possible, and keep your love going on and on and on . . .

Aries

You and your Virgo Guy will have a great time together, but first you'll have to be somewhat tame. If you come on to Virgo like the wild woman you can be, you could scare him away. He'll be looking out for your health first and foremost, and you'll provide him with sex that keeps him coming back, in more senses of the word than one!

In bed, your Virgo Guy will be mystified about what you do to him. Your strong, fiery nature will overwhelm him with passion. For a man who likes to hold his emotions in check, being with you in this way is a huge deal. The best part of this is, he'll want to reciprocate! His almost clinical way of finding the exact right spots on your body to bring you to almost instant orgasm will astound you.

To stay with your Virgo Guy, you're both going to have to be more patient. He'll have to live with your impulsiveness, and you'll need to deal with his occasional urgings to calm down, go slow, and let him love you.

Taurus

You will enjoy your relationship with your Virgo Guy because you feel so familiar to one another. You feel as though you're with your very best friend, and he feels protected and guided by you, as though he's with a great teacher.

In bed, things will also feel that way. Although the techniques he uses with you will take your body to some astounding heights of orgasmic pleasure, he'll need to learn a lot from you about sensuality. Your instinctive way of making love will bowl him over, and he'll pick it up from you right away. You may create a "monster," but it will be the kind you sure won't mind being in bed with!

You can trust him to figure out ways of keeping the house looking neat, although he'll often defer to you when it comes to doing the decorating. Together, you'll work out ways to be happy, comfortable, and free to let your love grow in the rich earth of your kindly hearts.

Gemini

You and your Virgo Guy will fall into couplehood with relative ease. You'll bypass your usual fear of being tied down with your Virgo Guy because of the way he respects your space. To him, you are an authority on many things, including how much time the two of you should really spend together. At the same time, he simply feels like "home" to you.

In bed, you'll have a blast practicing all the different techniques you develop. You'll find all the tender spots on his body, which usually involve his ticklish tummy. He'll learn how to talk about what he wants to do to you because he knows how quickly the words turn you on.

Let your Virgo Guy find a place for everything in your house and arrange schedules for you to take turns keeping it neat and clean. He'll be fair with that and easy to get along with in all things because the two of you have so much respect for one another.

Cancer

You and your Virgo Guy will have a sensational relationship because of the way you care for one another. You find it very easy to get used to him cleaning up around the house, while he loves the way you cook for him and always remember the things he loves most. Little romantic touches will do so much for both of you.

In bed, you have no problem getting used to his touch. He'll ask you questions about what feels good, and when you answer him, he'll make note of what works best for you. Eventually, you'll open him up emotionally because he'll feel comfortable with you once he sees you lay your heart out to him without reservation.

Don't mistake your Virgo Guy's matter-of-fact, down-to-business manner for a lack of love or devotion. Once he realizes how right you are for one another, he'll devote himself to your relationship fully and ardently. Although he may never be as deeply sensitive as you, he's thoughtful and kind, and definitely qualifies as the kind of partner you need.

Leo

Life with your Virgo Guy might not always be easy, but it'll be exciting and wonderful. It's really important for you to keep the lines of communication open. While you see him and the advice he gives you as a valuable treasure, you have an unusual effect on him. He often imagines that you don't like him, or that he isn't good enough for you. So, for all the constructive criticism he gives, he has just as much insecurity that you'll need to quell with gentle reassurance.

The best place to make your Virgo Guy feel more confident about himself will be in the bedroom. He'll know for sure he's truly loved by the wonderful way you devour his body, and he'll work hard to make you feel fantastic, too.

Around the house, he'll be the one to keep things clean, while you plan the social calendar. Division of labor and clarity in communication will help you make sure to get along for a lifetime of love.

Virgo

Life with your fellow Virgo will be a wonderful experience. Both of you tend to see life in the same way and deal with situations with the same set of skills. The only thing is, you'll have to avoid competing with one another. You might begin to believe you have to do things better or faster than your Virgo Guy, when in fact all you really need do is work together.

This is especially true in bed. Though you're both intensely sexually aware, you'll have to work a little harder at the art of seduction. Coming up with new ways to give one another pleasure will keep you happy and busy, but you'll also have to immerse yourselves in the act of making love to truly experience the sharing you intend.

Around the house, you'll probably both be neat and clean. You each have great home maintenance skills and good decorating ideas, and most important, you both want to build a healthy relationship. Keep talking and touching. You'll get there.

Libra

You and your Virgo Guy will have a very lovely thing going on. The two of you enjoy going out together, and you also pursue your separate interests. He sees you as someone who adds value to his life, while you notice the little things he says play on your mind, especially when he isn't with you.

In bed, though, there's no reason to do anything but be in the moment together. Your Virgo Guy is as eager to please you sexually as he is in your daily life. Let him lavish his considerable talents on you, while you give him pleasure by showing him appreciation for the great way he takes care of himself and goes that extra mile to remain sexually attractive to you.

Around the house, he moves around a lot more than you do, but if you let him do more than his share of household chores, resentment could build. Just like it is with the rest of your relationship, things are happier and richer when you work together.

Scorpio

Long-term love with your Virgo Guy can be a highly satisfying experience. He allows you to escape your deeply emotional existence long enough to look at the world in more practical ways. In turn, you bring him closer to his feelings than he'd ever go when he's left to his own devices.

The way you bring one another into balance is even more obvious when you have sex. Being together in bed is the best way for you to connect beyond the social level. Your deep emotions will be revealed in ways words can't really express, and your Virgo Guy could be moved to tears, no longer the cool, logical fellow you were talking to moments earlier.

Bringing each other out of your comfort zones will work for you even when it comes to taking care of the house. Let your Virgo Guy do the organizing, while you polish everything until it shines with the perfection both of you crave so much.

Sagittarius

Your love of laughter will be a huge help when it comes to life with your Virgo Guy. In truth, the two of you get along really well. You understand one another's motivations, and you realize he knows what he's doing. He, in turn, feels like family with you right away. He'll probably feel that his number one job is to protect you from yourself!

In bed, you'll be impressed by his knowledge of the human body and his sensitivity to what makes yours, in particular, "sing." The two of you connect through your hearts as well as your bodies, so you'll never get bored finding ways to be as close as possible.

Around the house, though, your Virgo Guy is going to teach you many hard lessons. Be mindful of and sensitive to his feelings about keeping his living space neat. Most of all, let him help you get organized, while you make him laugh far more than he ever would without you in his life.

Capricorn

It's such a relief for you to be with your Virgo Guy because it's easy to see how the two of you can make things work by combining your talents. Although you don't agree on everything, he sees you as his earthy, practical buddy, and you view him as someone who shares your opinions on most things that matter, especially morals, ethics, and the importance of tradition and custom.

Fortunately for your sex life, your admiration for his prim and proper nature stops there. Your life in the bedroom is far more untamed . . . and simply fun! Your Virgo Guy studies up on your body and registers every reaction you have to him, all so he can please you more every time you're together. Meanwhile, you give him permission to let loose and experience orgasm the way nature intended.

To your Virgo Guy, maintaining a home involves teamwork. While he might look to you to make long-term plans or manage bigger projects, he'll micromanage every last detail. If you admire strengths and he respects your ability to manage the big picture, you'll discover you really can be best friends, with enough sexual passion to keep you fired up for a really long time.

Aquarius

You and your Virgo Guy feel a very strong attraction, so focus on that as you do the rest of the work it will take to keep you together. You see your Virgo Guy as a highly sexual being, someone you can trust to share your body, mind, and soul with. He, on the other hand, views you as someone who can help him achieve his goals.

Not seeing each other in the same way doesn't mean you won't be able to have a gratifying sex life. You can achieve your most profound connections through nonverbal and very pleasurable communication. Make a point of ensuring your Virgo Guy enjoys himself, and you'll have a partner who'll go out of his way to provide awesome orgasmic experiences.

Around the house, Virgo's preoccupation with the details of neatness can be quite maddening, so be patient. Accepting your differences while working on becoming more alike might not be easy, but it'll help your relationship be more successful.

Pisces

You and your Virgo Guy view one another as ideal partners, but seeing what you want to see rather than what's really there can be a problem. The two of you must communicate on all different levels, all the time, to let your love reach its full potential.

Start with sex. While you get totally lost in your physical expression, your Virgo Guy is much more cerebral about making love. He's wondering whether he's pleasing you and how he can make you feel even better. Let him know he's doing fine by looking deeply in his eyes and expressing the complete bliss you feel.

At home, you're great at imagining how to best use a space, and an ace at decorating, while he focuses on cleanliness. Avoid clutter, and follow his schedule for cleaning up. When you recognize the major differences between you, it's easier to realize you're there to complete one another in very beautiful, soulful ways.

YOUR VIRGO GUY AND . . .

Staying with your Virgo Guy means you have to understand how he fits in to the various pieces of the puzzle that are your lives, and what you can expect as your relationship grows.

Your Female Friends

Your Virgo Guy will let you have your female friends and pretty much stay out of the relationships. Although he'll be curious about what these ladies do and some of the things you talk about when you're out, for the most part he'll be happy to stay home tending to one of his hobbies while you spend time with them.

Your Male Friends

Your Virgo Guy is going to be very trusting for the most part, so there won't be much controversy about your male friends. The way he sees it, if you say they're "just friends," that's all it is. There's no reason to avoid involving him with your guy pals, because he'll do all he can to make sure he blends right in.

His Female Friends

There's no doubt about it: your Virgo Guy needs to have some female friends. He wants to get the woman's view on many things in his life, from his work and the relationships he has there to how he deals with you. He'll only be trying to be a better partner through the benefit of his ladies' advice, so there's no need to think he'd cheat.

His Male Friends

Your Virgo Guy will have a lot of male friends, but rather than going "out with the guys," he's more likely to meet with them one on one. They might go to the bar or hang out at the gym together while they talk over their problems and compare notes. This is a healthy way for Virgo to vent so he stops worrying so much.

Your Family

Your family will probably think you've met the perfect mate when they're first introduced to your Virgo Guy. He's so polite, neat, and clean, and he can carry on conversations about everything from cooking to gardening to fixing a car in the garage. He'll enjoy seeing where you came from and be grateful that you share your kin with him. You'll be impressed by the way he tries to fit in without you even having to coax him.

His Family

Your Virgo Guy is always striving to do nice things for people, and this will of course be the case with his family. He'll be the one that fixes little things around his family's home, including the bruised egos of relatives worn from family battles. He'll also enjoy talking about family legends and sharing them with you.

Your Pets

Virgo has a special reverence and affinity toward pets and will love yours very much. Count on him to join in with you while you marvel at the cute things your pet does. He'll also be very supportive if and when you have veterinary issues and have an instinct for knowing what might be wrong and how it can be healed.

His Pets

Your Virgo Guy loves all living things and will almost always have pets around. He feels very much in tune with nature and recognizes animals' abilities to bring humans closer to their own animal side. While he'll like small animals such as dogs and cats, he might also like to spend time around larger animals such as cattle and horses.

His Potential for Success

Your Virgo Guy's career is likely to be consistent and profitable. He will make sure a steady flow of provisions rolls into the household. Although he might not be a corporate mogul or lotto winner, your Virgo Guy is a good worker, and his employers value him highly. One problem you might have is getting him to see beyond what he perceives as his limitations.

His Role as Father

While he makes a great dad, your Virgo Guy will be on the gentler side. He won't scold children loudly or make physical corrections to their behavior. He'll criticize them a lot, though. Although this can be useful when a child needs feedback, too much of it can damage little egos. Keep this tendency in check, if possible, so the little ones will remain respectful but self-confident.

VIRGO COMPATIBILITY

Your Sign	Compatibility Level
Aries	♈
Taurus	♉♉♉♉
Gemini	♊♊♊
Cancer	♋♋
Leo	♌♌
Virgo	♍♍♍
Libra	♎♎
Scorpio	♏♏
Sagittarius	♐♐♐♐
Capricorn	♑♑♑
Aquarius	♒♒
Pisces	♓♓♓♓♓

VIRGO SHORT-TERM PROSPECTS

Your Sign	Short-Term Prospects
Aries	♈♈
Taurus	♉♉♉
Gemini	♊♊♊♊
Cancer	♋♋♋
Leo	♌♌
Virgo	♍♍♍
Libra	♎♎♎
Scorpio	♏♏♏♏
Sagittarius	♐♐♐
Capricorn	♑♑♑
Aquarius	♒
Pisces	♓♓

VIRGO LONG-TERM PROSPECTS

Your Sign	Long-Term Prospects
Aries	♈♈
Taurus	♉♉♉♉
Gemini	♊♊♊♊♊
Cancer	♋♋♋♋
Leo	♌♌
Virgo	♍♍♍
Libra	♎♎
Scorpio	♏♏♏
Sagittarius	♐♐♐♐
Capricorn	♑♑♑
Aquarius	♒
Pisces	♓♓♓♓♓

CHAPTER 7

Libra (September 23–October 21)

YOUR MISSION: Present the Illusion That He Always Has Choices

Libra Potential Pluses

- Good-looking
- Diplomatic
- Gentle
- Refined
- Sophisticated
- Artsy
- Cultured
- Intelligent
- Tolerant
- Fair

Libra Potential Minuses

- Lazy
- Indecisive
- Procrastinates
- Not ambitious
- Prissy
- Detached
- Self-centered
- Overly romantic
- Insincere
- Wavering

WHAT THE LIBRA GUY HAS TO GIVE . . .

The graceful, elegant, and stylish Libra Guy has a manner about him that attracts you from the start. He has a way with others that leaves almost everyone believing he's doing exactly what they want. You might call him a "people pleaser," but most of those who are lucky enough to know the Libra Guy would consider him to be a master diplomat and genius at interpersonal relations.

He deliberates for a very long time before making his choices and often takes the easy way out when it comes to doing work, unless said work is exactly to his liking. Everything he accomplishes is done with one eye toward appearances. Two things are essential to his being: first, he wants people to like him, and second, he believes that unless someone else is there with him to watch and witness all he does, his actions have little or no significance. All of these attributes add up to create an exceptional, intelligent, and compassionate romantic.

As a Date:

Going out with the Libra Guy can be like participating in a fairy tale. He has a rather fantasy-laced idea about how the mating game should go. He will know the moment he meets the girl of his dreams; he will then kiss her; and then the two of you will live to love happily ever after. Alas, you might want to find out more about him first. He's a clever conversationalist, but also very evasive. He might never answer questions directly, at least not until he's certain you'll like the answer.

He might take you dancing or to a concert or even a museum. Venus, the planet that rules his sign, makes him a lover of the arts. If he decides he likes you, it'll be hard to miss the fact that with each of his words and motions, you're being seduced.

As a Sex Partner:

The Libra Guy can be sexy, but first and foremost, he's an unabashed romantic. He'll talk sweetly to you, stroke your hair and face with one finger, and then gently kiss you. If you're interested, just kiss him back. The slow and tenuous approach isn't about him not wanting you: it's all about determining if you like what he's doing. If you want to play with him, you can pretend to be unimpressed. This will make him work all that much harder, until you're genuinely thrilled with his performance.

When he sees you burst into orgasm, his heart will swell with self-satisfaction, because for the most part, he just wants to please you. His orgasms will be surprisingly explosive. Although he seems very refined, there's only so long he can hold back his hidden hotbed of passion!

As a Domestic Partner:

The Libra Guy appears to be a role model when it comes to being a life partner. He is a firm believer in the division of labor, and he'll quickly point out the ways it will be "fair" for you to split up the work that has to be done. Hint: usually that translates into a situation where you're doing the lion's share!

He's a fairly good earner, but don't look for him to have the kind of ambition that puts him into the category of "workaholic." You'll probably have to continue to pull your weight if you want to have the kinds of things Libra likes to keep around the house. You might think "nice vase," but he's got "Waterford" on his mind. The most beautiful and elegantly appointed items will be the ones he chooses. Budgets are minor inconveniences.

Emotionally:

Now, it can be hard to read the Libra Guy, who doesn't overtly express anger very often. In fact, many times he won't even act as though he's upset at all. Even though he tends to pretend that nothing bothers him, the Libra Guy does have feelings, and he acts on them. He'll become easily hurt if he feels there's something about him you don't like. Rather than using all that brain-power to rationalize and realize that might not be true, he'll plot out his response.

Look out though. Rather than argue with you, he'll assert himself in some backhanded way. The next time you slip on a banana peel, you just might find your Libra Guy nearby chewing on what used to be between those skins. When you ask him what you did to deserve it, he'll look at you blankly and glibly say, "Why, whatever do you mean?"

FIND YOUR LIBRA GUY!

You'll know that gorgeous guy you've been eyeing is a Libra by the graceful way he moves his body and sets his voice to a soft and unassuming tone. If you think he's checking you out, consider that he might just be scanning the room to confirm his suspicion that everybody's looking at him. In his magic mirror, he's definitely the fairest of them all. Approach him with a direct compliment about the way he looks. Once he stifles his reflex answer of "don't I, though?" he's likely to begin a rather fascinating conversation.

Libra's need for romance makes him easy to flirt with, but it can be tricky to get to know him. Look below to see how you can use the best attributes of your sign to get him close enough to touch.

Aries

You might not believe the Libra Guy is your ideal match, but in so many ways he is! He has an amazing amount of potential, but usually his talents take the form of ideas. Who or what can create the spark that motivates him to turn them into action? Why, *you*, of course!

He'll love the way you have this magical "I can do that" attitude, because in his world, there are always too many options to consider. You'll be enamored by his cool passivity, and delighted when he realizes you want him all for your own. You offer him a world of choices, because now you're there telling him how you can make his dreams come true.

His lack of motivation can get under your skin, but there are ways to get him moving. Leave him with the choice of doing nothing, but let him see that if that's what he decides, he's going to miss out on a whole lot of fun.

Taurus

You'll have to work with the Libra Guy to get him to become a more suitable match for you, but it can be done. The two of you are both prone to inaction; you dislike change, and he doesn't like to close off any of his options by making a choice in favor of another one.

You'll love it when he romances you with flowers or other little luxuries, especially chocolate! He'll admire how you seem to be able to acquire possessions and utilize your resources to get all the material things you desire.

If anything stands between the two of you, it might be the way he perceives you as chiefly a sexual being. You want him to know there's way more to you than that, and he has to earn your love. Making him put more of an effort into meeting your expectations will probably give you a better chance to create a relationship that will allow both of you to thrive.

Gemini

You'll spot the Libra Guy right away, because he'll be listening to what you're saying with rapt attention. The two of you share an intellectual bond that makes you almost constant conversationalists. He'll appreciate your observations, and you'll be awed by his ability to get along with virtually everyone he meets.

Both of you have a way with people, so many others may become peripherally involved in your relationship. Be careful about all those male "friends" of yours; the Libra Guy might not seem like it at first, but he's very much a one-on-one relationship person. He won't share you, at least not willingly. Also, you could quickly tire of his indecisiveness, and you'll often wonder why he can't just do what you like to do—which is everything!

Maybe you *can* convince him to be less of a deliberator and more of a doer. If you do, you'll have a companion with whom you can truly achieve a "meeting of the minds."

Cancer

You and the Libra Guy can get along well, but you'll have to set certain boundaries. While he views you as a person who knows more than he does about certain things, he doesn't want you to treat him like a child. Think of one another as family, but the kind of relatives you want to be around because you have so much fun!

He'll be right on board with the way you coddle and take care of him. Try not to overdo this, though. If Libra is left without anything to do, he probably won't do anything about it! Give him benchmarks and get him motivated. In other matters, you'll love the way he's soft and gentle with you, and he's definitely capable of tiptoeing around your deep and tender emotions.

Being with the Libra Guy, you'll soon learn that being nice to people, even when you don't want to, is almost always the best way to get exactly what you want.

Leo

There's an interesting interplay going on between you and the Libra Guy. You both are very concerned about and focused on your outer appearances, so there can be some competition. At the same time, you view one another as the kind of friend that's almost like a sibling. If you can tolerate the "sibling rivalry" part out of your inter-action, you have a great chance at creating a satisfying relationship.

You'll love the way the Libra Guy approaches you like a true romantic. He values your inner and outer beauty and rewards it with his sweetness and kindness. He'll admire your courage and strength and feel gratified that he can be with someone as unusual and out-standing as you.

Besides the possibility of jealousy, look out for his tendency to shirk his responsibilities. He'll happily compliment you while you do something to make his life easier, and he sits there doing what he likes. At least, even though he's manipulative, he's also terribly, temptingly cute.

Virgo

Your interest in the Libra Guy gives you a look similar to the gleam in a hunter's eye. Of all creatures available to you, this one seems like the one you want to "catch" the most. That's because you know he's incredibly clever, but also an underachiever.

Taking your Libra Guy on as your little project might be a good idea for both of you. You really do know what's good for him, and one day he'll show his gratitude for you not allowing him to get away with doing the bare minimum. He'll appreciate the way you seem to have your life in order. Still, you could grow impatient with his fixation on what's beautiful as opposed to what's useful, and he won't take too much criticism from you before he withdraws and stops talking to you. Be gentle with the kind knight who's also known as the Libra Guy, and he'll treat you like the princess you are.

Libra

Being with someone who's just like you could be very interesting! You'll both be very pleased to have a partner who understands what's really important to you in life, and why. Be careful not to assume that you're *exactly* alike, though. There's a possibility that you could have some differences that create some challenges.

You'll both love the romantic gestures that come so easily to each of you. He'll adore getting little tokens of love from you in return for the ones he sends *to* you. The one thing that you might have trouble with, though, is moving forward. From getting together to choosing spots for dates (or even calling for a break), you never seem to reach a final decision! When you seem to be talking in circles, a good friend or even a professional could help by playing referee.

Most of the time, though, the two of you will be very, very happy to be together. You'll create a world of love and beauty that will keep you smiling for a very long time.

Scorpio

While you're so determined to always be the best at what you do, the Libra Guy is happy to sit back and wait to see what happens. It may seem that you've met your "shadow," but that might not be the entire story. There will be times when the two of you are delightfully compatible. He sees you as someone he values, and he takes care of you like he would a precious flower.

Besides his lax attitude, your desire to be able to predict what he'll do next can get in the way of your relationship. He will always act like he's going along with you, but in fact the Libra Guy very much has his own mind and may dig in his heels until the last minute, especially if you press him to make a choice.

Still, the two of you can be very happy together, as long as you accept the elements that make each of you strong individuals. For you, this means that the act of "love" does not equate to "consume."

Sagittarius

He's stylish and refined, and you're boisterous and not so patient. Still, there's an attraction between you and the Libra Guy that you both know is the real thing.

He'll love your sense of adventure and think it's romantic of you to say "I love you" in fourteen different languages. You'll adore his ability to deal with people and tell them what they want to hear, even when it means he has to hold back on telling the whole truth.

Of course, there will be times when you grate at one another. You might not be able to sit still as long as he can, for example. If you keep waiting for him to suggest that you do something, you'll never get any action out of him. Take him by the hand, and show him what it's like to get engaged and active about life; he just might thank you! At the same time, you'll enjoy learning how to hold back those "unnecessary truths" that stand between you and true diplomacy.

Capricorn

You and the Libra Guy will have a very interesting relationship, but you each might not see it the way the other one does. To you, this is a "master-slave" relationship, and more than in just the kinky sense. You figure that, because you're so ambitious and powerful, the Libra Guy will spend his entire life making you happy. Now, he may make it appear to be that way, but most of the time he's doing what it takes to make sure you like him. He sees you as an authority figure he just can't resist duping, because it's an exercise in mental agility to get one over on you.

You'll admire his taste for the finer things in life, though—and he'll think it's fantastic that you have the resources to provide them. He won't steal from you, but you might wish he'd contribute more than he volunteers.

As long as you respect the Libra Guy for his considerable talents, you can form a lasting bond—clean or kinky, however you like it!

Aquarius

You and the Libra Guy understand one another perfectly. He wants to achieve balance and equilibrium between himself and everyone else he meets, and you want everyone to get along so the world can evolve to the next dimension. Okay, so in many ways you're from two different planets, but you can still build a strong relationship if you want one.

He'll greatly admire your intellect and your courage to laugh in the face of convention. You'll wish you could stop trying to stick out like a sore thumb long enough to emulate the appearance of grace and elegance that he exudes.

At times, you'll wish he weren't so fixated on getting people to like him, and he'll balk at your seeming lack of care about what anybody else thinks. Be more focused on what really matters: getting together as a couple and enjoying the great conversations that make both your minds soar toward intellectual ecstasy.

Pisces

Your romance with the Libra Guy will seem to fulfill many of the requirements you have for perfect love. For one, he'll approach you just the way you always hoped the most special man you'll ever meet would do. He's the kind who kisses your hand, opens the car door for you, and demonstrates the ultimate in manners and refinement.

He'll be fascinated by your creativity and your ability to adjust to just about any event that happens in your life. In your unassuming, almost naïve way, you can be singularly fearless.

The obstacle you face is the tendency for both of you to avoid living in the realm of reality. When you fail to remove your rose-colored glasses, you risk being blind-sided by the work you have to do in any relationship. Misunderstandings with the Libra Guy can be very confusing. Keep the lines of communication open, and you'll have a very easy time taking care of one another the way you should.

KEEP YOUR LIBRA GUY!

Now that you figure he's finally made the decision to be with you, how do you arrange your lives so he doesn't have any regrets about that? Let your Libra Guy know that he's loved and that you're there for him. This can often mean leaving it to him to choose which of the household chores he'd rather do, and offering him bilateral choices. "Eggs or cereal?" will be so much less of a problem for him than "What do you want for breakfast?"

Beyond his quibble with decision-making, you'll have to deal with his less-than-active physical tendencies. It really isn't out of line for you to suggest he can't get into bed with you unless he first fixes that squeaky door. Don't wait to see just how much mental energy he'll waste trying to figure out ways of getting out of it—or hoping you'll forget. You'll never believe it until you see it.

For tips on how you can use the charms and wiles of your sign to keep your Libra Guy, keep on reading!

Aries

Sometimes, the peace you perceive in living with your Libra Guy can seem somewhat unsettling. You're not mistaken! You do need to air your opinions now and then, especially when they differ. The trick you need to make this work, though, is to do so as quietly as you can. Your impulse to let off steam isn't going to produce anything useful, any more than his effort to sweep conflicts under the rug will.

Go to the bedroom to remind yourselves why it is you're together. He'll enjoy being taken over by you, as you set about to "conquer" him with passion. Meanwhile, he'll make you feel like a goddess, as he worships every inch of your body.

Around the house, look out for his trying to avoid the heavy lifting. Fortunately, an unsightly mess won't endure his desire for beauty and balance for long. Wherever you find yourselves, let him calm you down while you stir him up. That is the essence of your relationship!

Taurus

You can have a rather peaceful coexistence with your Libra Guy, most of the time. When you disagree, you'll need to be direct about saying what really matters to you. Don't prod or bully him because that could send him into a passive-aggressive tirade that makes you both unhappy.

In bed, you'll want to let your Libra Guy know you admire all the fabulous things about his body. His grace and beauty will astound you as he brings you to orgasm nice and slowly, the way you like it.

While you don't have to work too hard between the sheets, the two of you will need to put in extra time to get housework done. Make the process of cleaning your home a project plan, then stick to the schedule. That way you can evenly divide the labor and keep your environment so clean, you can easily make love in any corner of the house you choose.

Believing there are two sides to everything is a stretch for you, but being with your Libra Guy will prove it's true. Meanwhile, show him the aspects to beauty that are way more than just skin deep.

Gemini

You and your Libra Guy will enjoy being together because you're such good friends. One of the things you'll like the most about him is the fact that he doesn't want to manage and control you. He'll love the way you bring him new people to meet without his having to try too hard to make fresh connections.

Going to bed can take a long time for you and your Libra Guy. Because you both like to talk so much, it can take awhile before you close your mouths and open your arms. Once you do that, though, you'll have one very wonderful, masterful session of lovemaking after the other. After awhile, you'll both enjoy the challenge of communicating without words.

You'll both try to pretend you don't have to clean your home, but that won't make the dirt go away! Plan out a strategy for doing a little bit every day. In fact, giving the same kind of constant attention and vigilance to your love will be a great way to increase your staying power.

Cancer

Your Libra Guy will work with you to create a wonderful relationship. He'll provide all the sweet, romantic moments you can imagine, while you do enough nurturing and caring for the two of you. Just don't get too clingy or pushy . . . .

You'll cherish the chances he'll give you to shower him with affection in the bedroom, too. While he may not be as emotionally sensitive as you are, he does appreciate your professions of love and takes them very seriously. He worships the idea of two people living their lives as one and he'll work extra hard to do that with you.

Although you don't mind doing a lot of the cooking and most of the cleaning, you'll want your Libra Guy to do *something* around the house. You can probably get him to do light gardening—or supervise the landscapers! He thinks looking "pretty" is his job, and you'll admit he's darn good at it!

Leo

You might not be able to abide by much of what your Libra Guy does with his life, but you won't be able to resist the way he caters to you and strokes your ego with words of love. He always seems to know what to say to make you feel fabulous, and your presence alone is enough to turn him on. He sees you as a gateway to the wide world that responds to your magnetic personality.

In bed, as in the outside world, you can easily dominate and sometimes overwhelm your Libra Guy. Let him demonstrate his love and affection to you, too!

You'll almost never have a problem with him trying to outdo you on household chores. Your Libra Guy likes a nice environment, but enjoys it so much more when someone else makes it that way for him! You'll never be bored with so many things to talk about and negotiate, but if you open your huge heart to him, you'll always love your kind and gentle Libra Guy!

Virgo

Catching your Libra Guy is easy, but keeping him around may sometimes make you wonder what you got yourself into. He gets so distracted by what he's thinking, he forgets what he's supposed to be doing. Meanwhile, if you nag or make fun of him, he'll become deeply hurt. The way to get him to do his share of the work is to convince him that he is totally loved.

In bed, this should be easy. Your Libra Guy is likely very attractive, and even if he's not in perfect shape, there will be certain features that are extremely appealing. He'll charm you with his romantic touches, and soothe you when you're overwrought or feeling lonely.

For all these reasons and more, you'll forgive his transgressions, even when he shirks his duties. Though not entirely messy, your Libra Guy needs training before he becomes a help around the house. Keeping it peaceful with your Libra isn't easy, but this sometimes aggravating relationship is still worth the blood, sweat, and tears.

Libra

Have you ever seen a scale that's totally in balance? It doesn't move. All the tension in the air of one weight countering another seems to reach a point of peace, and all is well. So it is with you and your Libra Guy. The two of you get along perfectly, and all seems well, at least in your own little world.

Never is this clearer than when you're having sex. Your romantic expression is touching and endearing, and you each appreciate the other's effort to bring you to climax. You could stay in bed forever, feverishly working to express the love that you feel.

Around the house, though, you might not work so hard. You've got questions: Who will do the work? Who will cook and clean? The answer is, of course, both of you! Try to get motivated, though, before things get out of hand. Work quickly so you can go back to the safety, sexiness, and security of life in perfect equilibrium.

Scorpio

You and your Libra Guy will have an easy time keeping the passion flowing. He's such a romantic, and you're so sexy! He'll challenge you with his remarkable mind, and you'll keep him guessing as you use your uncanny emotional intelligence to read into what he's really thinking.

In bed, there's no doubt the two of you have a lot to say and do with one another. He enjoys watching you respond to his soft caress, and you seem to implode as a result of reaching climax via his smooth and charming sexual style. He not only enjoys watching you get off: he reaches new levels of excitement as a result of knowing he brought you to such a level of bliss.

If only he were so ambitious around the house! It isn't easy to get him to do his share of the work, but if anyone can do it, you can.

Dangling hot sex over his head will get him to do just about anything your deep and daring heart might desire.

Sagittarius

With the romantic Libra Guy in your life, there's not much you can complain about! He's handsome, sweet, kind, and good to you. He lovingly shares his life with you, and you have a feeling that no matter what happens, you'll always have a very deep friendship to share.

That's only one of the reasons why your sex life is so good. You and your Libra Guy have different ways of doing things, but you can always relate through the unique and bubbly way you make love.

You two will need serious help getting and keeping your house in order, though. Neither of you is a big cleaning person, so it might be a struggle to keep the place looking neat. In a most uncharacteristic way, your Libra Guy might be the one who takes the initiative to get things clean. You'll pitch in and give him an occasional hand, at least.

Helping one another and allowing yourselves to feel the love will be the way you keep your love affair going. Cherish the love you share!

Capricorn

You and your Libra Guy have an interesting sort of relationship. Although you're known as someone who wants to be "the boss," there are actually times when you'll look to your Libra Guy as a "higher authority." He does have a way with people that you just can't seem to muster up all on your own.

You know that because of what you feel when the two of you make love. He is more romantic than you are, but he can also be incredibly sexy. Because he'll do back flips just to make you groan with pleasure, he'll participate in the little games and contortions that truly turn you on.

Around the house, you could quickly become infuriated with your Libra Guy because of the way he puts things off, but all he'll have to do is flash that charming smile, tell you how well you do everything, and all will be forgiven. It's okay. You're not the only one who becomes a lump of helpless mush around your utterly disarming Libra Guy!

Aquarius

Your Libra Guy offers you a moral compass and shows you there is more than one way to look at an issue. His way releases you from grabbing on to an idea and never letting it go, even after it's proven wrong.

Liberation and release will be the themes of your sex life with your Libra Guy, as well. He'll take control of stimulating your body, and in his loving, caring way he'll propel you to a new level of sexual experience. In turn you'll light up with love for him, and do everything you can to ensure that you witness time and again how he retains his grace, even in the middle of an explosive orgasm.

Around the house, the two of you will need some supervision. A strict schedule for cleaning and doing laundry is in order. As the water bearer, you can take on scrubbing, while your airy mate mans the vacuum. When you're together, even during the glamourless moments, you will always shine.

Pisces

You and your Libra Guy are always smiling. By being together, you've taken two of the most romantic and peaceful personalities and allowed them to merge. One look at your Libra Guy and you melt into the universal love you strive for.

Sexuality is a spiritual experience for you, and for your Libra Guy, the romance involved in getting into bed with you is very precious. You'll work on making one another as happy physically as you are in other ways, and enjoy the thrills showing your love for one another can bring to your lives.

One of the items on your list of things to be done will be to remind your Libra Guy to pitch in at home. He doesn't have memory problems, but he'll deftly use that keen mind of his to work his way out of getting his beautiful hands dirty!

That's all right. When the chips are down, you'd rather those were clean when they're creating sensations all over your body.

YOUR LIBRA GUY AND . . .

Loving your Libra Guy will mean understanding more about how he'll react to the people and things you have in your life. It's also very useful to know more about how he allocates his attention when he's not with you.

Your Female Friends

Your Libra Guy appreciates the importance of all relationships, but he will also probably want to remain involved in some way. You want to go out with your girlfriends? He'll want to know where you and he will take them. Your Libra Guy doesn't like to spend time alone, so break it to him gently if you don't want him to come along.

Your Male Friends

Your "what" kind of friends? Libra might be somewhat emotionally detached, but when it comes to competition, he can get pretty fierce. At least at first, you should let him meet the guys you hang out with so he can be reassured you'll come home to him remembering your Libra Guy is the only one you truly love.

His Female Friends

The ladies have a hard time resisting your Libra Guy, and you'll have to share him without getting too jealous. He has the ability to listen to people's problems and help them solve them. The women you fear are hitting on him probably are asking him how to deal with their own guys. Chill. He'll be home as soon as he's done playing Dear Abby to the masses.

His Male Friends

Your Libra Guy will have a lot of male friends because he'll want to share his life and experiences with them. He knows there are certain things only a guy really understands. If he hangs out with a group of men, most likely there are one or two of them he'll identify as his confidantes. He'll always prefer that one-on-one interaction, even with his buddies.

Your Family

Everybody will love your Libra Guy around your house. His charm and elegance will almost always make a positive impression on your family. If he acts too formal or pretentious, encourage him to relax and enjoy the moment. He'll take some time to warm up and might appear shy until he knows no one is going to laugh at him or criticize him.

His Family

Your Libra Guy's attitude toward family is almost business-like. He won't really want to let you into the circle until he knows where your loyalties are. So, even as you try to make a good impression on the family, keep your Libra Guy between them and you. He wants to be sure that even if things go wrong, you'll still be at his side.

Your Pets

Your Libra Guy will be a bit indifferent to your pets, at least until he gets to know them and doesn't see them as threats. It's part of your Libra Guy's desire to want 100 percent of your attention, especially while your relationship is still being established. Later in the game, he'll take in Rover or Fluffy as part of you. Give him time.

His Pets

If your Libra Guy has pets, he will go for the kind that's not just cute but beautiful, too. In some cases, your Libra Guy could even get involved in showing his cats and dogs. With all that said, he also has a very spiritual connection to his pets and considers them to be part of his family and an extension of himself.

His Potential for Success

Your Libra Guy will do fine at work, once you get him up and out of the house. Even Libra Guys who have met with success have a tendency to rest on their laurels and not push too hard to take the next steps up the ladder. Still, there will always be just enough on the table, and maybe even more if you contribute too.

His Role as Father

In the natural order of things, Libra will be an adoring father, if not a particularly aggressive one. He'll fall for the kids in a "best friends" kind of way. This can be great when he's taking them to the park or getting them some toys, but when it comes to discipline, he might have a hard time mustering up the courage to enforce the "time outs" and grounding periods.

LIBRA COMPATIBILITY

Your Sign	Compatibility Level
Aries	♈♈♈♈♈
Taurus	♉♉♉
Gemini	♊♊♊
Cancer	♋♋♋♋♋
Leo	♌♌
Virgo	♍
Libra	♎♎♎
Scorpio	♏
Sagittarius	♐♐
Capricorn	♑♑♑
Aquarius	♒♒♒♒
Pisces	♓♓

LIBRA SHORT-TERM PROSPECTS

Your Sign	Short-Term Prospects
Aries	♈♈♈♈
Taurus	♉♉
Gemini	♊♊♊♊♊
Cancer	♋
Leo	♌♌
Virgo	♍
Libra	♎♎♎
Scorpio	♏♏♏
Sagittarius	♐♐
Capricorn	♑♑♑
Aquarius	♒♒♒
Pisces	♓♓

LIBRA LONG-TERM PROSPECTS

Your Sign	Long-Term Prospects
Aries	♈♈♈♈♈
Taurus	♉♉
Gemini	♊♊♊
Cancer	♋♋♋♋
Leo	♌♌
Virgo	♍
Libra	♎♎♎
Scorpio	♏
Sagittarius	♐♐
Capricorn	♑♑♑
Aquarius	♒♒♒♒
Pisces	♓♓

CHAPTER 8

Scorpio (October 22–November 21)

YOUR MISSION: Say Yes—or Be Forced to Say "Uncle"

Scorpio Potential Pluses	Scorpio Potential Minuses
• Sexy	• Manipulative
• Incisive	• Possessive
• Sensitive	• Demanding
• Perceptive	• Unyielding
• Intelligent	• Dictatorial
• Intense	• Secretive
• Determined	• Unforgiving
• Reliable	• Vengeful
• Attentive	• Unpredictable
• Inspiring	• Volatile

WHAT THE SCORPIO GUY HAS TO GIVE . . .

"Speak softly and carry a big stick" applies to the Scorpio Guy in more ways than one! This highly intelligent, quietly forceful, and astoundingly sexually charged guy is out to change your life! The Scorpion wins his disputes by stinging his opponent, and the Scorpio Guy follows his symbol's policy. As soft-spoken and unassuming as he seems on the outside, there is a stream of sheer power behind those piercing, incredibly intense eyes.

Yes, he's secretive, and when he does decide to strike out against someone, he uses the lethal force of the nocturnal ninja. His motivations, though, are usually rather pure. He is a great provider, and as long as you're on his side, the best kind of friend and supporter you could ever ask for. He will literally fight to the death for you. His sexuality is a bonus. His capability to transcend mere physical pleasure takes him and his lover through the gates of spiritual transformation via indescribable orgasms.

As a Date:

One doesn't merely go out with the Scorpio Guy: she is taken away by him. He will show the symptoms of being a control freak, but he really doesn't mean for his desire to achieve predictable outcomes to seem like he's trying to dominate. Besides, he feels he knows what's good for him, and you, too!

The best way to get him to look at you as an equal partner—rather than yet another person he has to "straighten out"—is to stand up to him. Tell him what you like and what doesn't please you. Once you gain his respect, you can start having fun. He'll take you somewhere that feels romantic and sensual and seduce you ever so slowly. Subliminal seduction through gestures, choice words, and other unconscious messages is something he probably invented long ago. Pitted cherries and bananas, anyone?

As a Sex Partner:

Even when he's calculating the probable outcome of one of his investments or project plans, the Scorpio Guy is thinking about sex. The act of merging with another person and creating the magic that has the potential to create new life is a constant preoccupation. You won't have any question about whether he wants you. Those piercing eyes will say it all. Once you get together, the magic will instantly begin. Everything you've ever read about in a steamy novel or seen in racy movies will pale in comparison to the experience you have with the Scorpio Guy. From his body's state of "endowment" to what he does with it, you'll be very favorably impressed. What will be even more wondrous is the way he gets lost in merging with you, and you willingly give yourself over to the act of loving him.

As a Domestic Partner:

The Scorpio Guy is as loyal as he is determined to succeed. Not only will he make sure you have what's needed in terms of material comforts, but he'll be there for you in every sense of the word. He'll stand up for you when someone challenges you and point out to you how you can do better when you haven't exactly put in the maximum amount of effort.

He'll prefer that your home be a quiet place where he can get rest and rejuvenate after the long days he's certain to put in at work. The colors that resonate with him—black and deep purple—might not look good on your walls, but they'll make nice accents that he'll love. He'll appreciate the little gestures you make to honor his tastes and show you love him as much as he cares for you, and guess where he'll show that gratitude. Lucky you!

Emotionally:

The Scorpio Guy is often misunderstood and accused of being nasty and mean. In actuality, he's ultrasensitive, sometimes moody, and always trying to do what's best for him and the ones he loves. He is very easily wounded because he often feels very alone in his quest for excellence, and in his loneliness he can appear to be a bit depressed.

His feelings of disillusion usually come from his experiences in the outside world. His disappointment in humanity as a whole makes his closest relationships that much more important. When he feels let down by those he loves, he can really go deep into an emotional hole. There's not much you can do except wait for him to thrash around and work his way back to a position of strength. That will be when people had better watch for his sting!

FIND YOUR SCORPIO GUY!

It really is true that the Scorpio Guy is always the sexiest one in the room. Even if he isn't the best dressed or the handsomest, there will be something about him that makes you want to get to know him better. His strong intuition tells him everything he needs to know about what you want, so don't even bother trying to hide your desire. You may have to put on the brakes if you don't want to be swept away into bed with him on your first meeting, though. When it comes to sex, the Scorpio Guy's motto is "Why wait?"

With so many other women competing for the perks of dating the Scorpio Guy, you'll have to stand out from the crowd. Use the following information to see how your sign can best join in with the Scorpion's tricky dance.

Aries

You'll find something to like about the Scorpio Guy right away. Although it might seem a little creepy that he's able to tell you what you're feeling and thinking before *you* even really know, you have to like a guy who's brave enough to read your mind.

If his attitude about chasing after what he wants seems familiar, it could be because the two of you share a ruling planet: Mars. You take Mars's daytime energy and use it boldly, while he absorbs the red planet's nighttime force and puts it to work under the cover of darkness and deception.

While you like to get things done fast, he will always work painstakingly until the task is completely finished. Just because he criticizes you for doing things differently doesn't mean he's always right. Try to work together as much as you can, and you can take the tremendous energy each of you has as individuals and transform it into a force of nature you can exercise as a couple.

Taurus

You won't be able to resist running over to the Scorpio Guy, and you might not realize you've approached him until he's up close and in your face! He exudes a magnetism that is completely irresistible to you. He knows you can't help yourself, so don't be embarrassed! In fact, he's just as attracted to you.

You're experiencing the sensation of being drawn toward the person who completes you in every possible way. The Scorpio Guy shares your slow and deliberate way of experiencing life. The two of you want to savor everything, especially each other!

While your ability to stand up to the Scorpio Guy and be just as strong and stubborn as he can be will ultimately win him over, it might take time for him to get used to it. He's not accustomed to anyone really being as strong as he is. Once he accepts this, though, he'll gladly embrace you and the two of you will get along fabulously.

Gemini

From your first meeting, you'll see that the Scorpio Guy is a bit out of the ordinary. He has a read on you and knows what you're up to right away. His first question might be whether you're really serious about talking to him, or whether you're just nosing around to see what he's like.

You'll love this seeming clairvoyance, and it'll be hard not to be drawn in by the sensuality that leaks from his pores. He'll be impressed by your ability to find out more about people, even when they don't seem to want to talk about themselves.

You'll find the Scorpio Guy isn't the easiest nut to crack in this sense and that could annoy you. Don't give up. Keep talking—even if he doesn't say a word—and give him time to build up trust. Eventually, you can have long, meaningful conversations and swap your impressions of all the people you meet.

Cancer

You'll pick up on the Scorpio Guy's vibe right away. His way of seeming to hide from the rest of the world is self-protective, and you totally get that. He'll be into you from the start because you seem so soft and gentle . . . and he figures he can easily take over your life and make it lots better!

You'll like the fact that he's strong, and you'll appreciate his ability to see into your emotions. He'll like the way you look up to him, and appreciate your sensitivity. He won't let you get away with brooding, though. The Scorpio Guy will never let you be a loser. You might not like the way he swoops in and takes over, but his desire to dominate doesn't necessarily come from bad intentions.

Your emotional affinity can help you build a sound and respectful relationship. Tell him how you feel, and he'll respect you. Once you realize that you're two people with a common purpose, you'll be well on the way toward emotional fulfillment.

Leo

You'll be attracted to the Scorpio Guy because although he's exceptionally quiet and inconspicuous, you sense his tremendous amount of personal power. He'll probably come up to you, smile, and not say a word. He wants to keep you wondering about what he's thinking.

While you'll admire the way he exercises his personal power, he can make you feel slightly uneasy. Yet, he'll be in awe of your style and the way you get people to follow you simply by flashing that megawatt smile.

You and the Scorpio Guy will do an odd sort of mating dance. The more you assert yourself, the less he'll come on to you. He'll make you want him, though, simply by standing there and giving off that unbelievably sexy vibe. He might try to make it seem otherwise, but he's very into you and wants you to follow him off to the nearest bedroom so you can let him show you just how much.

Virgo

Most people accept the Scorpio Guy as an enigma without trying to figure him out, but you're one of the few who's up to the challenge of solving the puzzle of his complex personality. You'll notice right away that he won't willingly tell you what he's thinking, but you won't let it get under your skin. He'll pretend he's not all that interested in you, but in truth, he can't wait to find out more about you.

He'll be fascinated by the way you can size up a person or situation and make recommendations for making things better in no time flat. You'll appreciate his desire to be the best at what he does, and you'll understand why he doesn't tolerate less than the best from everyone he knows.

You'll be more detached and practical than he. He often gets tied up in acts of revenge, merely because he can't separate himself from his emotional reactions. You can calm him down while he gets you more fired up and attuned to your ambitions. Plus, the fun, catty conversations the two of you will have will provide infinite entertainment!

Libra

You'll have a really high opinion of the Scorpio Guy from the moment you meet. The first thing you'll like about him is the way he notices you. You have a haunting effect on him that draws him toward you. You'll also note his ability to create a certain air of mystery about him, almost as if by magic, that just makes you want to be with him even more.

He'll like your way with words and admire the way you can detach from issues and analyze both sides. He'll slowly reveal to you sensual qualities that get you even more curious than you were to begin with!

His desire for excellence might lead him to prod you more than you might like, and your tendency to wait before taking action will drive him crazy. If you both decide this is worth the effort, being together will help both of you get better at the things you do on your own.

Scorpio

When the two of you are in the same room, you can't help but be drawn to one another. The Scorpio Guy, like you, exudes a certain sexiness that stirs up your own lust for love. You're capable of holding a whole conversation with just your eyes.

He'll like you because he knows you share his desire for excellence, and you'll find him to be just as strong and capable as you are. You'll both be strong enough to stand up to the other, and he has the same desire to assert his will as you do.

Hence, it could get hairy when both of you want to be in control at the same time. He won't always see things exactly the way you do, and both of you might try to force solutions more for the sake of getting your own way than because it's the way to go. As long as you remind each other it's better to be happy than "right," you won't waste time fighting when you can indulge in all that loving.

Sagittarius

You and the Scorpio Guy will have an interesting time when you first meet. You can't help but be yourself, even though some people will think you're a little loud and boisterous. He, meanwhile, will quietly examine your behavior, and most certainly figure out there's more to you than meets the eye.

He'll adore your sense of humor, but he'll like your intellectual curiosity even more. You'll wonder about his "mystery man" act, but you'll soon realize a lot of this is shyness. Be careful about offending him; his emotions are very delicate, and his temper can be volatile.

The subconscious messages he sends out put you more in tune with his feelings than you normally would be with someone else. Try not to run away, even when he makes motions that convey his desire to possess you as well as to love you. In time, he'll learn to give you more space to roam. Give each other time to build up the mutual trust you need to achieve and sustain lasting love.

Capricorn

The Scorpio Guy will intrigue you right away because he's so sexy. He'll strike that chord within you that sets off your most animalistic urges, and you could even forget about everything that's happening at the office—if only for that one moment.

He'll like the way you organize and motivate others. He'll like to listen to you talk, and although he may not say very much, he'll be forming his opinion. He won't be able to ignore your sexual proclivities, and this relationship could quickly lead to a one-night stand or a façade of a partnership that's really based more on sex than love.

If you want it to be more than that, you'll have to open your heart and mind to becoming more sensitive, and he'll have to use his rather keen intellect to separate himself from pure emotion. There's a bit of work to be done, but nothing the two of you can't accomplish, especially if you do it together!

Aquarius

You and the Scorpio Guy have a lot in common. You'll notice one another right away because you tend to stand aside from the rest of the crowd and have no desire to "fit in." You'll also assess each other's sexiness and how you turn each other on with a familiarity that seems to be there even before you speak.

You'll like talking to Scorpio, because you can see him take in everything you say with his deep and soulful eyes. He might not say much to you at first, but that won't seem to matter. He'll adore hearing all your perceptions of the world and how you think it can be made better. He'll agree with you most of the time, at least long enough for you to get close enough to have sex!

There's no doubt about what the Scorpio Guy is after, and he may want it sooner than you do. Don't be afraid to tell him where your boundaries are. If he realizes just how "worth it" you are, he'll keep chasing after you, and once he catches you, neither of you will want to let go.

Pisces

You might not believe the Scorpio Guy is "a Scorpio" when you first meet him. He won't seem nasty or secretive at all. On top of that, this mystery man shares with you an incredibly high emotional IQ.

He'll love your creative side and the way you have magnificent visions and such an eye for art. You'll adore his ability to perceive what's going on inside other people's heads before he even starts a conversation with them. More than anything, you'll appreciate his suggestions for organizing your life better. You know you need his kind of advice.

Keep the lines of communication open in both directions, though. If you delve too deeply into your nonverbal way of conveying your feelings, there are some risks. Either or both of you could begin to see and hear what you *want*, rather than what's real. Better that you know for sure where each of you stands, and that's more than likely to be together!

KEEP YOUR SCORPIO GUY!

Making your relationship with your Scorpio Guy last requires dedication and to some degree, submission.

There's no question that your Scorpio Guy loves sex, and yes, you can keep him around simply by being there for him in that way. Still, there's a lot of depth to your Scorpio Guy, and unless you stand up to him and meet him on his own terms, he's going to get tired of you rather quickly. Laziness and lack of ambition don't register well with this guy.

You'll also have to stay out of some of his business. Although your Scorpio Guy isn't really "secretive," he is private. Even you have to be kept out of the loop sometimes. When he's ready to trust you, or he's sure it's important to you, he'll tell you everything. Until then, just give him his space. He'll show his appreciation by being your strongest supporter and probably the best lover you'll ever invite into your bed!

Once you've decided to dive into life with this mysterious and attractive guy, you're going to need some inside information about how your sign's built-in radar can help you navigate his complicated personality. Read on to get savvy about your special way of engaging in the Scorpion's dance.

Aries

You and your Scorpio Guy need to communicate your needs clearly. There may be times when he "shows" you how he feels rather than tells you. If you can learn to read him: great. If you think you're missing his point: come out and ask him what his problem is . . . nicely. A sampling of your temper won't do much besides provoke him, and you won't want to do that, especially not close to bed time!

The way you and your Scorpio Guy make love is the stuff of legends. Your strong and straightforward style is met with his all-encompassing, coddling adoration. He does more than *have* sex: he savors it. He'll teach you how to go slow and enjoy every minute of it, too.

Around the house, you'll both be bossy, but between the two of you, the housework will get done. What's important is having the space and time you need to be the active people you are and sharing your lives so you can enjoy everything about one another.

Taurus

You and your Scorpio Guy are instant love mates. You'll settle in rather easily, after a few disputes over who will be allowed to put what where. Keep remembering he's not used to someone actually standing up to him with the same amount of determination you have, so when he doesn't get his way he could get pretty broody!

Cheer him up by insisting you have sex immediately! He'll love the way you cherish every second of your lovemaking time. He'll be deeply passionate, slow, and deliberate, just like you! There's a lot to be thankful for with your Scorpio Guy in your bed, but you already know that!

His behavior around the house will be rigid, but you can get him to do at least some of the housework. Remind him he's not the only strong and stubborn one around, and he'll pick up his end of the load. Your love for one another is so special, you'll enjoy doing anything as long as you're together!

Gemini

Actually making a commitment to your Scorpio Guy is going to be a scary proposition for you.

Once you go to bed together, that will all change. You'll see that for all his attempts to control you, all he really wants is to be loved, and to show how much he loves you. By the time he's done, you'll do almost anything to keep having sex with your Scorpio Guy! That's not all there is to your relationship, though. The intense conversations you have will be a huge intellectual turn-on. He'll constantly question your ideas and challenge your opinions.

At home, your Scorpio Guy loves to think he's getting one over on you, so if he gets you to take out the trash when it's his turn, he figures he's scored a point. When you get fed up, call him on it. Eventually, he'll realize that there has to be give in take in all areas of your relationship, and you may even earn enough respect to get him to let you go out with the girls once or twice a week.

Cancer

Moving closer to your Scorpio Guy is going to be a joy for you, for the most part. There will be times when you wish he could be more accepting of your varying moods, but he won't! Get used to him telling you to pull up your bootstraps or to stop being so crabby.

All he really wants is for you to be nice and stable so you can get down to what he thinks is really important: being in bed with you. You might never tire of being loved and pampered by someone who knows exactly how to make you happy, from head to toe.

You might even buy into his idea that you do all the housework, but if you're quick-witted, you'll see what he's up to and make him do his share.

Loving your Scorpio Guy, giving into him when it's appropriate, and making him do his part for your couplehood will form the perfect mixture for setting you on the road to long-term love.

Leo

Your life as your Scorpio Guy's reason for living will suit you well. Although he won't buy into your need for almost incessant attention, he will acknowledge you're someone very special! You'll have to agree that he has some uniquely admirable attributes, too.

His way of sharing bodies is something far beyond the usual mutual stimulation. He creates an atmosphere between the two of you that leads to a feeling of transformation. You go to bed as one person and end your lovemaking session as another after a spiritual experience.

When it comes to housework, he may not treat you like the royalty you are. It can be difficult to get him to participate in the nitty-gritty of housecleaning. Gently remind him there's only so much one can sweep under the rug! Then, after he's done with the dusting, walk over to him and lock lips in one of those electric kisses. Your love is all your Scorpio Guy ever really needs.

Virgo

You and your Scorpio Guy have a great thing going on, especially when it comes to talking things through. You're both after the same thing: making each of you better so you can be as close to a perfect couple as possible. Treat him with the same respect you'd want, and you'll be off to a great start.

In bed, there's no reason to talk about much! Your Scorpio Guy knows instinctively all the things you've studied over the years. You can learn how to "let go" more when you're with him, because having sex with him is like riding a bike without training wheels for the first time. Wheee!

Around the house, he won't be terribly messy, but he will resist your urgings to do the housework. Maybe you can put together a schedule and give him actual assignments, due dates, and times. When he's working toward a goal, there's no stopping him. That's one of the many reasons why the two of you have such a great life together.

Libra

Your diplomatic nature diverges greatly from Scorpio's "all-or-nothing" attitude, but if you work on that with him, he might come to believe that even he is in need of improving a few things about his personality.

His sexual style doesn't need a whole lot of work, though. He seems to know every last thing that's going to make you scream with delight, while being with him gives you a magical ability to increase his potency and urge him to orgasm when you're both ready.

Around the house, he'll be the one pushing for the work to get done, and he'll want you to do it. He'll show you how things "should" be done, so if you have different ideas, you'll have to prove they work better. Your Scorpio Guy will always push you to try a little harder, but because you're so graceful, beautiful, and loving, he'll let you have just enough leeway to keep you hanging around.

Scorpio

You and your matching partner will probably have an easy time finding your way into being a lasting couple. You both want the same thing: excellence! You'll seek it out in every way and provide for one another the things you would want for yourselves.

This will go double for your sex life. The two of you making love is an experience most people would envy! Each of you will take turns touching all the right places, and you'll savor the way it feels to be so close to someone who seems to know everything about you.

The games you play around housework will get pretty interesting! You'll go to great lengths to get your Scorpio Guy to do more than you, but be careful: he's watching your every move, and plotting out his way to get revenge. Staying together can be challenging, but when being together is so much fun, it gets easier. Take your life one day at a time. The years are bound to fly by when you're having so much fun.

Sagittarius

Getting closer to your Scorpio Guy may be a bit taxing for you. While you do feel very attracted to him, you still have a fear of him taking over your life. This could be because he's so powerful, emotionally as well as physically. It could also be due to your desire to have enough freedom to enjoy life's little adventures, and yes, sometimes *alone!*

When you think about what it's like to have sex with your Scorpio Guy, though, you might change your mind completely. He has such an endearing way of tending to your every need and finding every last bit of your body that creates sexual sensations you simply can't forget.

Your Scorpio Guy would much rather be doing anything else but housework, but he will expect that it gets done and hold you responsible. Make him accountable for doing his part. You can do it! He'll believe you, especially when you tell him it's the right thing to do!

Capricorn

You're powerful, so how is it that your watery, emotionally burdened Scorpio Guy can have such a great hold on you? He can seem to read your mind and yet be mystified by what you mean when you try to tell him something he needs to improve.

Sex is one area of your relationship where you'll have to admit he's got it right! His high-octane sensuality caters right to your nearly insatiable desire. He wants it as often as you do, and at times, even more intensely. No complaints in the bedroom!

The rest of the house could get pretty messed up, unless you do what it takes to make sure he helps you out with it. He'll try to manipulate his way out of doing the dirty work, so assign him details such as vacuuming and keeping the car as clean and pristine as he likes it.

Don't give up on trying to get Scorpio to "behave." You're one of the few people who can command his respect. Once he sees how capable you are, he won't mess with you at all!

Aquarius

You and your Scorpio Guy will be very secure and happy together. He'll eventually see he can't control you, and you'll come to realize he can be right about your need to open up more emotionally.

Work on these issues in the bedroom. Although you like to think you're cool and detached about relationships, your Scorpio Guy will show you there's a better way to go. He'll open your heart by creating sensations in your body you can only describe as "spiritual." And, once you look deeply into his soulful eyes, you'll realize his love is very real.

Around the house, you might have to demonstrate your egalitarian ideas to him and show him what a great thing it is to pull together to get things done. Okay, so you're shaming him into getting his hands dirty, but he'll find it hard to resist doing everything it takes to please you!

Pisces

You'll enjoy life with your Scorpio Guy! He's going to make you feel secure, and he'll be strong enough to protect both of you should anything happen to threaten you as a couple.

Your sex life will be a glorious celebration of the transformative powers of nature. You're right with him when your lovemaking propels you to a higher plane. Although this isn't all that will keep your relationship together, at least you can depend on make-up sex to end silly spats.

Housework could be something you quibble over, but it'll be up to you to make it seem more fun for your Scorpio Guy! Create a sequence of cleaning that can be worked out to music—or try it naked! Always appeal to your Scorpio Guy's need for unusual stimulation and sexy situations, and you'll keep him close for a long, long time!

YOUR SCORPIO GUY AND . . .

As your love grows, you and your Scorpio Guy will eventually have to come out of the bedroom and deal with daily life. Read on to see how Scorpio's attitude about different people and things in your life might strengthen or challenge your relationship based on your sign.

Your Female Friends

Your Scorpio Guy finds nothing wrong with you having female friends. He'll respect your need and desire to have other people to talk to who share your perspective on life. If you have conversations anywhere near within his earshot, though, you can count on him listening in. He's just curious, but if you say something he doesn't like, you could be in trouble later.

Your Male Friends

If you really want to tell your Scorpio Guy you're going somewhere with some male friends, wait until your relationship is firmly established. He isn't going to want anyone else to be near you, nor is he going to want any other man to get the chance to talk you out of spending almost all your time with your Scorpio Guy.

His Female Friends

You don't have to accuse your Scorpio Guy of always being fair. Just because he doesn't like you having guy friends doesn't mean he can't have a few who are girls. After all, he knows *you* can trust *him*! He enjoys female company because it gives him perspective on what women like. So, you see, he's only doing research so he can learn to create some happier times with you!

His Male Friends

Your Scorpio Guy will be rather popular with his male peers because he knows what they like and makes sure they all go somewhere to enjoy it. Although he probably won't cheat on you, your Scorpio Guy will have a tendency to talk about your sex life with his buddies. It's nothing personal; he just has to brag about scoring with a winner like you!

Your Family

Your Scorpio Guy might not impress your family right away because he keeps to himself so much. Encourage him to be himself around them because you just know your family will accept him! If that's doesn't work out, then let your Scorpio Guy take the lead and use his instincts. That interpersonal radar of his will zoom right in, and he'll be able to tell when he's safe.

His Family

Your Scorpio Guy's family relationships can vary from the manipulative to the fabulous, but your job is to stay out of them. Let him take the lead and navigate through his family network at his own pace. He really does know best about who he can trust and who's going to be good to you. Simply smile and accept you're just along for the ride.

Your Pets

You have a special, psychic connection with your pet, so your Scorpio Guy will try to make friends with this creature. Since this is also what he wants to have with you, he's going to follow your pet's cues. He'll also watch the way you treat your pet and size you up that way. There's no escaping Scorpio's scrutiny, and your pet will love the extra attention.

His Pets

Your Scorpio Guy's pets will be strong and noble animals. He won't want just a cat: it'll be a black cat with the will of a lion. His dogs are likely to be of the as-scary-as-they-are-noble variety. He'll gravitate toward guard dogs and others that have the kind of teeth no one wants to encounter in a dark alley.

His Potential for Success

It's likely that your Scorpio Guy will have a comfortably profitable career. He always makes sure there are enough resources to feed and clothe everyone in the house, and he probably has a secret stash somewhere so you'll all be covered in the event of a rainy day. He can become very wealthy, but he won't sell himself out to work at the expense of your relationship.

His Role as as Father

Your Scorpio Guy will strive to be the best dad on the block, and he will get pretty darn close. He takes child-rearing very seriously, and will work with each child individually to discover and develop his or her potential. He is patient but not tolerant of laziness or bad behavior. He's the kind of dad kids might not "like" while they're little, but they'll grow to appreciate his wisdom and love.

SCORPIO COMPATIBILITY

Your Sign	Compatibility Level
Aries	♈♈♈
Taurus	♉♉♉♉
Gemini	♊♊
Cancer	♋♋♋
Leo	♌♌♌
Virgo	♍♍
Libra	♎
Scorpio	♏♏♏
Sagittarius	♐♐
Capricorn	♑♑♑
Aquarius	♒♒♒♒
Pisces	♓♓♓

SCORPIO SHORT-TERM PROSPECTS

Your Sign	Short-Term Prospects
Aries	♈♈♈♈
Taurus	♉♉♉
Gemini	♊♊
Cancer	♋♋♋
Leo	♌♌♌
Virgo	♍
Libra	♎
Scorpio	♏♏
Sagittarius	♐♐
Capricorn	♑♑♑
Aquarius	♒♒♒
Pisces	♓♓

SCORPIO LONG-TERM PROSPECTS

Your Sign	Long-Term Prospects
Aries	♈♈♈
Taurus	♉♉♉♉
Gemini	♊♊
Cancer	♋♋♋
Leo	♌♌♌♌
Virgo	♍♍
Libra	♎
Scorpio	♏♏♏♏
Sagittarius	♐♐
Capricorn	♑♑♑♑
Aquarius	♒♒♒
Pisces	♓♓♓

CHAPTER 9

Sagittarius (November 22–December 20)

YOUR MISSION: Love, Laugh, and Let Live

Sagittarius Potential Pluses

- Curious
- Adventurous
- Brilliant
- Fair
- Protective
- Colorful
- Open-minded
- Culturally aware
- Enthusiastic
- Generous

Sagittarius Potential Minuses

- Unpredictable
- Late for everything
- Unreliable
- Too intellectual
- Distant
- Restless
- Clumsy
- Tactless
- Naïve
- Gullible

WHAT THE SAGITTARIUS GUY HAS TO GIVE . . .

He's a little untamed, he's outrageously funny, yet he's cultured, well read, and curious as all get-out. The Sagittarius Guy is just like his symbol the Centaur. Half man, half wild animal, he embodies the discovery, capture, and refinement of his element, Fire. His search for truth will lead him on a long, curvaceous, bumpy, and thrill-packed road through life. If you're lucky enough to travel some or a lot of it with him, expect action, adventure, and impetuousness from this playful guy.

He has a genuine love of life that you must always support and encourage. Your ability to stay positive will appeal to him. He can be a good provider and reliable partner, but he must follow his personal passions. The gratification of his intellect and the fulfillment of his desires to have fun will always come first. Remember these things and you will reap the rewards of a very happy life with the Sagittarius Guy.

As a Date:

Want to attend a lecture being offered by one of his retired college professors or try windsurfing? By saying "yes" to the Sagittarius Guy, you'll be signing up for a date that's sure to be fodder for many tales to tell your gal-pals later! When he decides he likes you, he'll come on strong, but don't misread this as a big ego. Actually, he's sort of shy and has to push himself past his fear of you saying "no" in order to walk up and invite you to talk with him. He rarely keeps a very exact schedule because he wants to be open to fun stuff that might happen on the spur of the moment. You might see lots of comedy flicks while craning your neck in the front row because he was late (again), but at least you'll giggle together!

As a Sex Partner:

If you like puppy-love kisses and exuberant displays of affection, then you'll love having sex with the Sagittarius Guy. He's pretty upfront about what he wants from you, but he won't really want to have too much of a discussion about it. Start out assuming that he's thinking "no strings attached," because more than anything, Sagittarius values his freedom. This doesn't mean you can't have an exclusive relationship, but allow him some latitude when it comes to him following his dreams. The last thing a person as honest as this wants to do is cheat on you. While he's away, he's probably sampling some wild delicacy like fried grasshoppers or steamed sea urchin, or doing something else you'd rather hear about than witness. Think of his reading and travel as opportunities to pick up sex secrets from around the world!

As a Domestic Partner:

To say the Sagittarius Guy doesn't think much about cleaning up after himself is a kindly understatement. Because his life moves so fast, you'll often see a trail of clothing left in his path, and areas of the home that are "his" will be arranged in what he might refer to as an "organized mess." If you're not willing to clean up after him, this could lead to more than a few disagreements. The easiest ways around this would be to call on a cleaning service or set physical areas of the house apart so he can unleash his animalistic housekeeping habits somewhere outside your field of vision.

He's a very loyal person, and although words such as "marriage" and "commitment" literally frighten him, you have to move into your relationship at his pace. Once he trusts you won't be restricting his freedom or stifling his curiosity, this Sagittarius puppy dog will be yours to keep!

Emotionally:

Sagittarius is much more emotionally intelligent than he appears on the surface. The factor that drives his feelings is The Truth. He will often stick his own neck out in order to make sure others don't lose their freedom without cause. If a wrong has been done to him, Sagittarius will feel it deeply. He's unlikely to seek revenge, though. Because he likes to be nice, he'll hope that karma or some other mystical force ensures the offender is forced to pay for the crimes committed.

If you happen to upset him, he'll retreat. It's easy to forget how hard it is for the Sagittarius Guy to settle down. When he runs off, though, it's a sure sign you need to apologize and do whatever it takes until he knows he can trust you to provide the unconditional love he's seeking.

FIND YOUR SAGITTARIUS GUY!

He could be the one who's telling a joke to a small cluster of enraptured listeners, or the focus of an intense conversation that seems way too serious for the social scene. Part of the Sagittarius Guy's charm is his diversity; the rest is his puppy dog-like innocence. He's easy to get to know, but more difficult to pin down. The Sagittarius Guy is on the move both mentally and physically, and if you want to get with him, you're going to have to start by holding up your end of the conversation, and understanding how precious freedom is to him.

This one isn't easy to get, and he's even harder to keep, but he's ever so easy to love! Take a look at what your sign's special talents and tendencies can do to help you attract the simple-yet-fascinating Sagittarius Guy.

Aries

Like the kindred spirits you are, you and the Sagittarius Guy will be extremely excited to meet each other. You'll know by the way the conversation goes that this is someone who's capable of keeping up with you and approaching life with the same level of passion.

You'll love how he's willing to go to the ends of the earth for an adventure, and he'll admire your enthusiasm and leadership. Your tastes will be very similar when it comes to most things, and he'll be even more adventurous than you. Sometimes, he might wonder why you choose to go head-to-head with people just for the sake of doing battle. You would do well to adopt his attitude of being more adaptable, while he will learn the art of fighting for what he believes in rather than just discussing it.

There's no doubt life with the Sagittarius Guy will be fun for both of you. Take turns coming up with new adventures, and you'll never tire of it.

Taurus

Meeting the Sagittarius is a shock to your system, but it can also be a wake-up call of sorts. While you might balk at some of the things he does for fun, such as skydiving or scuba diving, some part of you wishes you could let yourself go and do these things too.

Honesty and integrity mean a lot to you, so you'll really like the Sagittarius Guy's focus on the truth. He'll appreciate the way to protect what is yours, and admire the way you always finish what you start.

He won't necessarily be able to emulate you, though. One thing that could drive you mad about him is the way he's working on so many things at once. In turn, your fixation (or what he might view as "obsession") with one thing at a time will get on his nerves. If you open your mind as well as your heart, you could easily zipline and parasail your way to happiness.

Gemini

You and the Sagittarius Guy will find each other immediately, no matter how crowded your first meeting place might be. You'll recognize his sharp focus on the things that capture his interest, and most likely, one of them will be you.

He'll love the way you zip through the universe, chatting and smiling, passing a little ray of sunshine on to people wherever you go. You'll admire the extent of his knowledge, and respect him for being smart enough to know there's always something left to learn. You complete one another by merging your two worlds of ideas.

While it's great that you've both found someone who's happy to let you have your freedom, you'll need to be very deliberate about finding time to do some things together.

In general, keeping the focus on life as a pair will be easier when you both take a deep breath and make the commitment to stay in one spot long enough to give love a chance to grow.

Cancer

When you first meet him, you'll just want to run up and hug the Sagittarius Guy. His sincerity, his hilarious sense of humor, and the fact he needs more than a little mothering will combine to make him incredibly attractive to you.

You'll fall in love with the way he'll defend people so that the truth can prevail. He'll admire your ability to hold down the fort, even when the world around you is all crazy and chaotic. Most times, he will say exactly what he's thinking, and this can sometimes hurt your feelings. He doesn't mean to be rude; the truth just leaks out of his mouth before he has a chance to polish it up and make it palatable.

Don't let a few verbal faux pas send you away from what you have to gain from being with the Sagittarius Guy. He can open you up to a world of adventure that turns life's merry-go-round into a cutting edge thrill ride you can learn to love.

Leo

You and the Sagittarius Guy will like one another right away because you share a vibrant and lively way of expressing yourselves. While he's not as fixated on helping individuals develop their talents the way you are, he does have a very strong interest in spreading knowledge so people can live life to the fullest.

He'll love the way you come right out and speak your mind, and you'll admire his willingness to learn new things, even if it means he must humble himself to do it.

While you're not so great at admitting your weaknesses, he's a little bit too blunt for you at times. This can be worked out by talking about the way you each feel when either of you doesn't think before you speak.

You and the Sagittarius Guy will make a dazzling couple, and although it could take a long time to get him to settle down, having a dashing, brilliant, and funny partner by your side will be well worth the battle.

Virgo

The mixture of conflict and confluence between you and the Sagittarius Guy can make for interesting fireworks, even at your very first meeting. This "you say tomato" kind of relationship might seem unworkable on its surface, but when you get to know each other, that can change dramatically.

You'll admire his talents and desire to experience just about anything so he can learn, and he'll wish he had your ability to analyze, organize, and prioritize. Before long, it'll be easy to see how this can become a "two heads are better than one" situation, too.

He might not like how you insist on everything being "practical." In turn, you'll find his messiness to be maddening and wonder how he can possibly function in the midst of chaos. Let each other do what you do best, and you'll be in charge of putting order to the disorder that results when he brings home ideas that broaden your consciousness and expand your mind.

Libra

You and the Sagittarius Guy have an easy time talking and getting along. You view him with a familiarity that lets you understand where he comes from, while he appreciates your friendship from the outset.

He can't help but admire your way of making peace, even when the people involved in conflict seem to be divided by irreconcilable differences. He'll cherish the experience of being surrounded by your beauty, too. Meanwhile, you'll be fascinated by his thinking and get easily wrapped up in his exciting, if wild, way of life.

You might not be too enamored by some of the things he says. He can be reckless, careless, and a bit clumsy. Meanwhile, he won't want to kiss up to people he doesn't trust, and won't like it when he sees you deal with people that way. Rather than trying to be the same, appreciate the different ways you look at the world and be grateful you've found one another. You have a tremendous amount of love to share!

Scorpio

Your first impression of the Sagittarius Guy might not be all that positive, but as you get to know one another, your connection will get stronger. At first, he seems brash and almost disingenuous. Is it really possible for someone to be that upfront and honest? At the same time, he'll be wondering about you. Why don't you talk more, or at least give your opinions out loud?

Stick around, and you'll see that yes, the Sagittarius Guy really can be that happy and optimistic about what he sees as the truth in his life. He'll also grow to admire your depth and your integrity when it comes to pursuing excellence.

The love of knowledge might be one thing that really keeps you together. As two seekers are prone to do, you might often have conflicting perceptions, but you'll offer a wealth of information and insight to one another, too. Before long, you could be bungee jumping just for the fun of it!

Sagittarius

What will two Sagittarius people like you need when you first get together? Adult supervision would be a good start. The two of you are so boisterous and outrageous that the clatter you make when you're talking and laughing together could fill the whole room.

You'll love his way of being upfront and honest with you, and he'll be so psyched to find out he's found someone who'll willingly, happily, go on life's many adventures along with him. Work on the idea of commitment, though. If you leave too much room in your relationship, one of you could easily slip away.

Staying together will mean a great deal of fun and excitement for both of you, so remain focused on that. Don't worry too much about the future, and enjoy every day you spend together. Before you know it, you'll create a safe relationship space that also gives both of you the space you need to grow.

Capricorn

Your first encounter with the Sagittarius Guy might not be entirely pleasurable for you. Although you like his sense of humor, and find him to be entertaining, there's something about him that makes you uncomfortable. It could be his wild streak, or the way you feel he goes to too many places and sees too many things to have a clear view of any of them.

You'll like his curiosity and admire his adherence to truth and justice. He'll like your ability to see the big picture and how you organize people and tasks so the job can get done.

Your desire to fit him into a more practical way of life could make the Sagittarius Guy feel constricted, though. Try to respond to his wild-and-wooly side with your often concealed untamed sexuality, and the two of you might have a lot more to do with one another than you first thought.

Follow him on an adventure, and you might not want to leave his side ever again.

Aquarius

The ideals you and your Sagittarius Guy share will probably be revealed in the first few minutes of your conversation. You believe people have much more potential than they use, and you see it as your respective missions to wake them up.

He'll love your visionary attitude and appreciate your ideas for making the world a better place. You'll adore his fiery spirit and enlist his help to inspire people on a more individual basis.

You might draw the line at some of his physical exploits, though. While you can get into the idea of a nice glider or air balloon ride over the wine country, getting involved in hunting, camping, or long-distance running sounds just a bit too risky to you. Your reluctance to join him will only add to his basic fear of commitment.

To stay together, the two of you will have to be willing to experiment with one another's ways of having fun. Release your inner "wild child."

Pisces

You're gentle and sweet, and that's the first thing the Sagittarius Guy's going to like about you. The two of you will hit it off, maybe because neither of you ever feels really comfortable in a crowd. You'll both be glad to find someone who's fun and easy to talk to.

You'll be very impressed by the Sagittarius Guy's ability to do so many things at once. You share this adaptability with him, and he'll note that, as well as your considerable creative talents. The differences in the way you approach people could create static between you. Although he's very caring, he's also direct to the point of being insensitive. You'll have to tell him about your feelings and how easily they get hurt, and also try to toughen up just a bit, because he means no harm.

Let your Sagittarius Guy make your dreams come true. Why just sit around and imagine going on an adventure when this dashing man will sweep you up in the real thing?

KEEP YOUR SAGITTARIUS GUY!

When you think about what it's going to take to stay together with your Sagittarius Guy, always allow him the freedom to be who he is.

The minute you try to tame the wild animal side of him, the human side will stop growing. He can become indolent and self-indulgent, probably in an effort to get you to dump him so he can be free again! He doesn't want to see other women, necessarily. He just wants to be free to go out with the boys or take trips by himself, so it's just him and the rest of the world he wants to learn about.

Your Sagittarius Guy values unconditional love. He will certainly offer that to you, and expect that, in spite of his messy manner and lack of tact, you'll love him no matter what happens. Because he's loyal, honest, interesting, and so much fun, this really isn't a very hard job at all.

To make it even easier to stay happily together with your Sagittarius Guy, read below about how the qualities of your sign will mesh with this wild child's irresistible personality.

Aries

Life with your Sagittarius Guy will be filled with excitement and enjoyment. The two of you have a childlike quality that allows you to immerse yourselves in life and come up smiling every time. As long as you make the time you need to be together as a couple, you'll discover that when you share experiences, they can be even more intense.

This will certainly prove out in your sex life. The only problem you two will have is deciding who will be the one making the conquest here. You both enjoy the ritual of winning the other one over so you can share your fiery, passionate love, so why not just take turns?

Your house will need more attention than you might think, thanks to the busy lives you both lead. You'll need a storage area for sports equipment, and the creativity to make cleaning your living space into a game you can both play. Always keep the "fun" there, and you two can last forever!

Taurus

After you've struggled to get your Sagittarius Guy into your life, keeping him there shouldn't be so hard. Consider how much time you'll have to yourself when your Sagittarius Guy is out learning, traveling, and otherwise expanding his field of knowledge.

When he comes home, you can be waiting for him in bed. He'll eagerly join you there and let loose with some of his more animalistic traits as he ravishes your body. You'll provide a place for him to be where he knows he'll always be accepted and loved.

Even though he's not the neatest guy you'll ever meet, he's great at tasks such as yard work and snow removal in the great outdoors. Leave lots of leeway for him to pursue the things you don't want to be bothered with, but do join him for the occasional trip or lecture. You'll learn a lot from your Sagittarius Guy, and he'll adore the stable environment you provide for him.

Gemini

Life with your Sagittarius Guy is going to be a lot more enriching than you even imagine. The two of you share the desire to think and talk as much as possible, but that won't be the only things that you do well.

Your sex life will be illuminating. Even if a spiritual awakening is the last thing you have in mind while you're taking off his clothes, by the time you're done making love, both of you will explode with the ecstasy of becoming as one.

Cleaning up around the house after your Sagittarius Guy won't be so pleasurable. His lack of reverence for physical possessions is just one more thing for you to love, hard as that might be to remember when you're wiping cookie dough off your MP3 player. There are prices to pay for loving and living with your Sagittarius Guy, but you'd gladly pay double for the joy he brings you.

Cancer

Adjust your expectations for hours of togetherness with your Sagittarius Guy. He will want to be out and about just as much as you want to be at home. Compromise with him, and you'll get it right.

Sex with your Sagittarius Guy could be one way to get him to spend more time around the house. Be the savage seductress you can be, though, rather than the nurturing, mothering type. He likes a little coddling, but if he starts to feel smothered by you or the too cushy surroundings you tend to create, he'll bolt out of there like the lightning he's always chasing down.

Let him help you cut down on clutter, while you encourage him to remember it's easier to find things like keys and wallets when they're put away nicely rather than strewn wherever they land.

Gentle talk in both directions will help you foster this relationship, as will a lot of time holding hands, gazing at the stars and then into each other's eyes.

Leo

You'll ease right into life with your Sagittarius Guy because the two of you have a natural appreciation for adding spice into your lives.

You'll enjoy listening to his ideas and going on trips with him to find interesting places to make love.

No matter where it is that you go to bed, you'll always have a very happy sex life. Both of you are fervent about the way you express your emotion. He'll also have poetic ways of describing your beauty and how privileged he feels to be in your regal presence.

Around the house, send your Sagittarius Guy outside to do some of the heavy lifting. He'll happily do what you ask, but rarely takes the initiative on caring for his things and putting them in their proper places around the house. This is part of life with your Sagittarius Guy. Like a good curry or tangy tomato sauce, it can get messy, but the combination of spices will create an exquisite mixture.

Virgo

You and your Sagittarius Guy have a nice arrangement: you keep one another in check. While he's constantly exploring and collecting information, objects, and experiences, you're analyzing what you have in front of you and sorting through what will be the most useful and practical elements to keep in your life.

No doubt, when you and your Sagittarius Guy are together sexually, you'll get right down to the bare essentials. He's highly passionate, and you're more than willing to explore his body to find where and how you can give him the most explosive orgasmic experience possible.

Around the house, frankly, he'll drive you crazy. But while his lack of neatness and decorum grate, he'll also give you permission to loosen up, and maybe come to believe that there really is such a thing as "an organized mess."

Libra

You and your Sagittarius Guy might not always be at peace with one another, but he'll definitely get you up and moving. His desire to be out and about as much as possible will challenge you to pick up the pace of a life you normally prefer to let pass you by.

Your Sagittarius Guy has a way of igniting sexual passion that surpasses even your idea of what a romance should be like. He won't give up until he substitutes your passive attitude toward sex and turns you into a wild-eyed, orgasmic maven.

His way of keeping house won't add to its beauty, but it will give it charm. You probably won't clean it up for him, hoping he might, but don't wait too long. Tell him when you've reached your limit, and he'll do what he must to improve appearances. There's not much he won't do to keep you, his beautiful princess, loving and caring for him for as long as possible.

Scorpio

You'll enjoy life with your Sagittarius Guy as long as you can work on building the kind of mutual respect you need to keep your love affair going. Face it: you're good at emotional instincts and perseverance, and he's a fantastic and courageous explorer.

You'll discover this in the bedroom, to be sure. While you're intensely sexual and fixed on pleasing your one and only love, he can be overly excitable and easily distracted. Most of his problem is a fear of being literally "consumed" by you and your relationship. Always let him know where the exit door is, but cherish him so he would never think of using it.

Around the house, you'll have to deal with his boisterousness and a basic lack of awareness about where his body and his belongings are. Help him, but don't enable this behavior. He'll learn that getting his act together is part of the job of pleasing you, and that's all he really wants—to make you happy.

Sagittarius

You and your matching Centaur mate will have a wild and crazy time together. The good thing is, you'll always have a buddy who's as daring and brave as you. On the negative side, the two of you will have a hard time paying enough attention to business while you're out there having all that fun.

Your sex life will be fantastic—when you stop long enough to enjoy it, that is! No matter where you are in the world, taking the time to be with one another in this way is always going to help keep you together.

As for your house, the only way you'll keep it clean and neat is to admit defeat after you've both lost the ability to find the floor. Face up to your deficiencies in this area, and approach cleaning as you would any other subject you need to learn about. After all, you always want to create space for making love!

Capricorn

You and your Sagittarius Guy will seem like a mismatched pair to other people, but the two of you know what each has to offer and wouldn't want to be with anyone else.

Your sex life is one reason why you love being with your Sagittarius Guy so much. His passion and willingness to explore all the avenues that lead to orgasm make you glad he's your partner. His animalistic side creates an "anything goes" atmosphere in your bedroom that you will always welcome.

Your Sagittarius Guy will need some house breaking if you want to have a peaceful spot in which to live. Your way of preserving order will make him feel constrained, so offer the option of his own room or a closet where he can keep excess items.

As long as you're willing to allow him the time to explore the world, your Sagittarius Guy will come back to you every time because he knows you offer a touchstone of sanity for him, along with the best sex ever!

Aquarius

Awakening the masses can be a tiring job, and your Sagittarius Guy will feel your pain. The two of you share a view of the world that pushes you to always make things better, no matter how bleak they may appear. You'll also have fun going places other people wouldn't put on their travel itineraries because you're more interested in learning than indulging yourselves in decadent pleasures.

The one exception to this will be in the bedroom. You and your Sagittarius Guy both enjoy sharing your bodily pleasures, so always rent a room that's big enough for both of you to sprawl out.

Your Sagittarius Guy will need your help when it comes to taking care of the house. Set up a structure for him and make some rules, but don't be too strict. The secret to your happy relationship is to always leave enough physical and mental space to your individuality for both of you to grow.

Pisces

You'll be so happy with your Sagittarius Guy! You both like to learn new things about the world and have an unconventional approach to your daily lives. He likes to spend a lot of time out of town, or at least around town, which leaves you enough space for your individual pursuits, from daydreaming to meditation class.

There will always be a happy reunion in your bedroom. You and your Sagittarius Guy are both extremely tender-hearted. He is as innocent as you are and is so glad he can trust you not to play with his emotions. You appreciate the way he respects and protects you.

You might be the one person capable of integrating Sagittarius's random way of keeping house into your home décor. He'll clean up when asked, so don't be bashful about (gently) reminding him to pick up his stuff. He'll be so glad he's making you happy, and you'll know that your life is better, richer, and lots more fun with your Sagittarius Guy in it!

YOUR SAGITTARIUS GUY AND . . .

There will be times when you and your Sagittarius Guy will have to come up for air and deal with the rest of the people and things you have in your lives. Read on to discover how being with your Sagittarius Guy will affect some of your other important relationships.

Your Female Friends

Always trying to get your attention with his jokes, your Sagittarius Guy will look for funny things to say about you and your female friends. He won't want to go out with you, necessarily, but he'll be excited to hear about what you did while you were away. He never minds these girls' nights out, because that leaves him time to just be free.

Your Male Friends

Your Sagittarius Guy will be rather tolerant of your male friends. He's a live-and-let-live kind of person, and he figures that if you wanted to be with someone else, you wouldn't keep coming back to him. Don't even think about trying to get him jealous; he'll just smile with the realization of knowing he's had you all along.

His Female Friends

Your Sagittarius Guy is bound to have some female friends because he doesn't really make much of a distinction between guys and girls in his platonic relationships. The kinds of girls he likes to hang with will be very excited to meet you and will probably want you to hear some of the reasons why they like him so much as a friend.

His Male Friends

Your Sagittarius Guy has a large posse of male friends, and they do some pretty wild stuff together. From going to the ball game on a weeknight to spending weekends in the woods, you're going to have to let him have his moments while he's out being part of his tribe. Imagine the bear hug he'll give you when he toddles back home!

Your Family

Your Sagittarius Guy will rely on his sense of humor when interacting with your family, whether they're comfortable with it or not! They'll come to love him, of course, because they can't resist his impishness and his ability to tell stories and teach them things while having such a good time doing it. They'll all love him without fail, and you'll learn to appreciate your family more because of him.

His Family

Even if his family wasn't the most perfect set of relatives he could have asked for, your Sagittarius Guy will try to be good to them. Depending on the people they are, his family might not support his constant traveling or his quest for education even after many years of study. Your job is to pump him up in front of the folks and keep that smile on his face.

Your Pets

Your Sagittarius Guy loves animals, and he figures the wilder they are, the better. So, if you have that puppy that's just a little bit out of line, or even something less conventional such as a ferret, he'll really take to your pet. Your being these pets' constant companion tells him that you have your own wild side that he will love.

His Pets

Your Sagittarius Guy might not have furry friends in his house because he could be afraid they'll get in the way of his travel plans. He might also decide that he'd rather visit wild animals, either in their natural habitat or on farms or in zoos. Horses will be a favorite for most Sagittarians. He'll love letting his hair blow through the wind as the horse gallops onward.

His Potential for Success

Your Sagittarius Guy can be a good provider, but he can also be more sporadic in his earning patterns. He's not a slacker, but he can lose interest in his job and stop trying to get ahead in the world. He can also move from one field to the other until he's found one that won't leave him feeling creatively stifled and physically penned in.

His Role as Father

Your Sagittarius Guy is going to have a lot of fun being a father! He'll get down on the floor and play with the little ones and teach the more grown-up ones about sports. He'll even help out with homework! He will provide a very strong, positive role model, and with his humor and his giving nature, keep the kids giggling (or rolling their eyes) like crazy.

SAGITTARIUS COMPATIBILITY

Your Sign	Compatibility Level
Aries	♈♈♈♈
Taurus	♉♉
Gemini	♊♊♊♊♊
Cancer	♋♋
Leo	♌♌♌
Virgo	♍♍♍♍
Libra	♎♎
Scorpio	♏♏
Sagittarius	♐♐♐♐
Capricorn	♑♑
Aquarius	♒♒
Pisces	♓♓♓♓

SAGITTARIUS SHORT-TERM PROSPECTS

Your Sign	Short-Term Prospects
Aries	♈♈♈
Taurus	♉♉
Gemini	♊♊♊♊♊
Cancer	♋♋
Leo	♌♌♌
Virgo	♍♍
Libra	♎♎
Scorpio	♏
Sagittarius	♐♐♐
Capricorn	♑♑
Aquarius	♒
Pisces	♓♓♓♓

SAGITTARIUS LONG-TERM PROSPECTS

Your Sign	Long-Term Prospects
Aries	♈♈♈♈
Taurus	♉♉♉
Gemini	♊♊♊♊♊♊
Cancer	♋♋
Leo	♌♌♌♌
Virgo	♍♍♍
Libra	♎♎
Scorpio	♏♏
Sagittarius	♐♐♐♐
Capricorn	♑
Aquarius	♒♒♒
Pisces	♓♓♓♓

CHAPTER 10

Capricorn (December 21-January 19)

YOUR MISSION: Respect His Authority

Capricorn Potential Pluses

- Organized
- Reliable
- Strong
- Capable
- Diligent
- Serious
- Sexy
- Intelligent
- Ambitious
- Urbane

Capricorn Potential Minuses

- Detached
- Demanding
- Distracted
- Distant
- Old-fashioned
- Opinionated
- Strict
- Decadent
- Unfeeling
- Calculating
- Materialistic

WHAT THE CAPRICORN GUY HAS TO GIVE . . .

This intellectually sharp, practical, and effective man knows what he wants and rarely stops going after it until it belongs to him. His symbol, the sea goat, is a creature capable of going to the deepest depths and the highest heights in order to achieve his goals.

Capricorn tends to conceal emotions because he fails to see practical reasons to deal in the realm of feelings. This doesn't mean he hasn't got the ability to connect with people, because in fact he is extremely loyal and becomes deeply attached to those he loves. He treasures his family and respects tradition. The Capricorn Guy has it within his power to deliver all the good things in life and strives to do so for the benefit of the people he loves, especially his partner and the family they create together.

As a Date:

Your first few dates with a Capricorn could feel like a job interview, but don't put on a front. Just keep being yourself. The Capricorn Guy will detect any attempt to hide behind a fake personality, and dump you promptly if he does.

Capricorn will always keep his promises. If he's interested, you'll know. When he says he will call—he will. If he doesn't, he might call someday, but by then you might not be as interested as you were before.

Trying to jump the gun or push him into a relationship are tactics that should be avoided. He will see you as being desperate and needy, and these are two things he does not want to see in you, because he doesn't want to take total responsibility for your emotional well-being. Be an original!

Capricorn is cold on the outside and reserved on the inside. Yet, in his own way, he's definitely lovable and affectionate. For instance, he might not be the first one to jump up and hug you to say hello when you meet in public, but once you're all alone and he shows you how glad he *really* is to see you, it will feel like you're the luckiest woman in the world.

As a Sex Partner:

In the bedroom, you're sure to find out what anyone who's been intimate with a Capricorn Guy will tell you—he's *red hot!* Most Capricorn men will tell you very directly what they want to do, how frequently they expect it, whether they want it fast or slow, and if they think you need more practice at it.

But he's also more likely than most men to ask what makes *you* feel good. If you're too shy to tell him, let him experiment! He'll revel in taking possession of the magical controls that transform your body and its aura into a panoramic burst of color—a screaming, howling, heavy-breathing, toes-curled climax machine!

His orgasms are far more explosive—and consciously released—than those of many men, much because the Capricorn Guy is willing to wait for the exact, right moment. He likes to be in control of everything— especially getting out of control!

As a Domestic Partner:

Around the house, the Capricorn Guy may appear to be a clueless man-child, not too great at cooking, and the last person you'd expect to be able to sew on his own buttons. Don't worry. He takes his laundry to be done, and probably earns more than enough money to make dinner reservations. As for home repairs, he lets the professionals deal with that stuff, too.

Because Capricorn is so involved in work-oriented, status-building activity, he needs you to do the little things that make his life easier, like making sure his power suit is cleaned and pressed for the big presentation. He doesn't ask for a lot, because he wants to prove he can take care of himself, and cater to your needs, too!

Emotionally:

You already know how the Capricorn Guy tends to conceal his emotions, but what might surprise you is just how loving, tender, and vulnerable he can be. He cares much, much more than he tends to show, so be gentle! He wants to know he has your respect.

Even if he does something to deserve it, never refer to him as a "typical man." If you want him to act like a Neanderthal, he will—just to show you who it is you're toying with. Although it's hard for him to utter the words "you have hurt my feelings," he has other ways of showing it. When he becomes broody or begins to make snide comments about you in front of your friends, start apologizing. Eventually, when he feels you have become open, exposed, and maybe contrite enough, he'll tell you exactly what's making him feel unloved.

Once he's processed an unpleasant experience, a personal slight or an ego-crushing comment, Capricorn will bounce back into your relationship from a much more pleasant and sunny emotional place.

FIND YOUR CAPRICORN GUY!

The Capricorn Guy is a stickler for the rules. His strong sense of the way things "should" be comes from Saturn, his sign's ruling planet.

Structure, custom, policy, and procedure are necessary components of his interactions, even when it comes to love. To him, the man is the aggressor, and the woman, though valuable for what she has to offer, is the one who must be ready to receive his affection and sexual passion.

The Capricorn Guy will figure you're interested in him when you ask him questions about his work, comment on what a great leader he is, and leer at him lustily from across a crowded room. He'll be attracted to you if you have a distinct sense of style and show the ability to be a strong individual, yet are flexible enough to mesh into his world. If you're patient, and if you prove to be worthy of this man's attention, no one else will do a better job of treating you like a real, live queen!

Getting the Capricorn Guy to notice you will be much less daunting when you understand what he wants, and how the characteristics of your sign will convince him you're more than well worth his time.

Aries

Introduce yourself to your Capricorn Guy by pointing out the many things you have in common. You're both self-starters, independent and capable of doing just about anything you put your minds to. Show him some deference, especially when he points out how your impulsivity is something that you're going to have to curb.

Patience is something that comes to him easily, but it's not infinite. You'll have to demonstrate that you're willing to learn from him, and offer to teach him some things he might not be so adept at, such as taking a leap of blind faith—hopefully, into your arms. He'll admire your courage, and appreciate the way you're open to trying anything just because it's different and new—especially in bed. If you can accept that he'll always try to be the boss, and he can understand your need to express your ideas and opinions, the two of you will totally enjoy being together, no matter what you're doing.

Taurus

The Capricorn Guy will make an immediate, positive impression on you because he satisfies many of the items on your list of things you like in a man. Feet on the ground? Check. Got a good job? Yep. Prosperous? Usually. Because you're so solid and protective, you offer Capricorn the kind of safety and security he feels he deserves. However, you might have to get over being so stuck in your ways.

Although he'll admire your ability to stick to a project until it's done, he may not always agree with the painstaking pace at which you go through life. Also, although he likes the nice things in life, he's far more frugal than you'll ever be. Bend a little, and you'll get a lot from being with a Capricorn Guy.

Keep telling him how much you depend on him, and watch his confidence in his importance in your life grow and grow. As long as you can accept his need to be the boss, you won't have much to complain about. What can be wrong with having a nice, reliable Capricorn Guy to spoil you rotten?

Gemini

At first, you and the Capricorn Guy might wonder what, besides a rather intense sexual attraction, has brought you together. There's no denying that this refined-looking creature does something to turn you on. You seem to be able to see through all his pretentions, right into his wild side!

He'll notice all your admirable traits, but there will also be a kind of disconnect between you. While he's always centered and focused on one thing at a time, you like to flit about and get involved in as many different conversations and interesting interpersonal interactions as possible. There's no doubt, the Capricorn Guy is high maintenance, with a big need to get attention and praise for the noble things he does in his quest to woo you.

You're not all that easy to pin down, and this will make you all the more appealing to the average Capricorn Guy. More than most, he enjoys knowing he's got you to do something you didn't know you wanted to do. You'll come to relish all that calm, sound advice from the Capricorn Guy, as long as he leaves you a long enough leash.

Cancer

You and the Capricorn Guy are naturally compatible, as each of you fill the other's desires for love and affection. You want someone to appreciate what you do to create a sound home and family environment, and he's looking for the right person to inspire him to great achievements in the area of hunting and gathering.

Let your similarities build a bond between you, while your differences complement your positive points. He may not always be totally sensitive to your emotions, but you have to understand how he doesn't pay that much attention to his feelings. Any symptom of you becoming controlling or too needy will send him running for his favorite place: the hills.

Despite the fact he might not fully believe in "soul mates," he'll know he's met his the moment he lays eyes on you. Play it cool, though.

He'll lustfully grab you, throw you over his shoulder, and take you home with even more pride and joy if you are a bit coy!

Leo

The Capricorn Guy intrigues you because you firmly believe you deserve the best and are pretty much convinced he can offer it to you. In turn, your self-assured manner will turn his head immediately, and he will see you as a vibrant, lustrous sex goddess.

The best way to get his attention is to admire his potential for sexual prowess. Even if this isn't your first motivation for getting closer to him, as time goes on you'll find that his ability to satisfy you is a definite plus! This man sees you as a most magnificent, but wild, animal—and won't be satisfied until he has you totally tamed.

His reserved nature might make him seem a lot wimpier than he really is, so don't be shocked when Capricorn begins to make demands on you. If you pretend like you don't mind his suggestions, he'll continue to worship the ground you walk on. Keep your own levels of drama down. The minute you show signs of becoming high maintenance, his illusions and imaginings of a life of lust and love with you will be shattered forever.

Virgo

You'll be impressed at how the Capricorn Guy seems to have his life perfectly in order and respects your ability to tend to details while he takes care of shaping the big-picture events in life. You may see him as your best buddy, but he views you as a teacher. He'll be thrilled at the way you seem to master sexual techniques and talk about them so openly. He'll view your clinical approach to this and many other areas of life as a practical, common sense way to approach them.

Before you construct a labyrinth of rules you must live by, though, consider the fact that the Capricorn Guy will always try to trump your authority. He might use his wry sense of humor to let you know who he considers to be the boss in your relationship, and you can be sure it isn't you. He'll dole out just as much "constructive criticism" as you do; with a great deal of love and respect, of course!

Libra

His gentlemanly manner, secure station in life, and ability to sweep you off your feet with his pure, earthy manliness are just a few of the things you can't help but notice about the Capricorn Guy. It's true he's the perfect candidate for Prince Charming, but you'll have to hustle to fit into that glass slipper.

He'll admire your intellect and be a captive listener, as long as your ideas have substance to them. He'll see through any sort of false "charm," as his practical manner forces him to cut to the chase before you get finished trying to construct some beautiful illusion for him to fall in love with.

He represents home to you, while to him you're a prize he'll boast about. Never let him forget that you have allowed him to choose you, and he'll continue to love and respect you for a very long time.

If you want to seal the deal with him, be more decisive. He won't want to wait around while you endlessly deliberate about what to wear on a date, so make a choice quickly, and he'll put you on a pedestal forever.

Scorpio

The Capricorn Guy will impress you from your first glance, because he won't be afraid of you. However, this is an extremely difficult man for anyone to dominate, and that goes even for someone as artful at manipulation as you! From the inception of your relationship, *you'll* need to concede that this man is at least your equal and make *him* believe you think he's your superior.

Capricorn will admire your ability to be self-sufficient and your desire to be the best. You work together as a formidable team, as long as you let him take the lead. Think about how great it might feel to have a partner to take responsibility and make decisions!

The Capricorn Guy will respect your need for privacy, and he will try to keep a few secrets from you too. He'll want to remain somewhat a mystery, as you do, so there will be just enough tension to create an atmosphere of excitement and titillation you're both going to thrive in.

Sagittarius

Although you may not be quite as grounded as the ambitious Capricorn Guy, you'll still be fascinated by his ability to turn just about anything he touches into gold. You'll also appreciate his wry sense of humor and the way he uses it to try to win you over and into his bed, most likely by the end of your first date. The Capricorn Guy will be amused by the way you're always thinking about something, and be impressed that you want to learn something new every day. Sometimes, though, he'll wish you'd stop thinking and studying long enough to enjoy the material aspects of life.

Capricorn is more than capable of taking care of you, but first you'll have to become open to letting him do it. He might try to change his ways so he at least believes he's giving you all the freedom you want. Let him in on your plans, but don't neglect your impulse to roam the world for new discoveries. Encourage him to come along with you and share the adventure!

Capricorn

You'll pick out the other Capricorn right away. Who else could possibly share the same impeccable taste and dashing appearance? You won't be surprised to find out that's not all you have in common. Although you both like the finer things in life, you're not overly extravagant. You'll agree on most matters, even the "taboo" subjects such as sex, work, and politics. Most of the time you're together, you'll probably be thinking about at least one of the three!

He'll like the way you can handle his powerful personality without being intimidated, and he'll appreciate it when you don't challenge his reserve when it comes to overtly expressing emotion. Yet, you'll be deeply attracted to one another. With all this mutual admiration going on between you, it's clear that you and the Capricorn Guy will be on the same, steamy page right away!

Aquarius

The Capricorn Guy is as cool as you are, which will be a huge turn-on. You know what you want, and so does he; and neither of you gets bogged down by emotions or irrational behavior. From your first meeting, you'll be relieved to detect this isn't one of those scenes that suffers from an overabundance of drama.

He'll love listening to you talk, but he might not buy into all your ideas. Meanwhile, you could quickly get annoyed when you notice his tendency to be materialistic. If you can learn to accept one another's points of view, you'll find that being together is mutually rewarding.

You inspire him to think beyond the bottom line, and he encourages you to keep at least one toe on the ground.

You won't have to look hard to find there's a wild and crazy side to the Capricorn Guy that you'll just adore. For all his prim and proper gestures, underneath he could turn out to be the kind of naughty boy you could easily learn to love.

Pisces

The Capricorn Guy is so strong, focused, and grounded! You'll notice he's a lot of things you sometimes wish you could be, such as serious, organized, and able to make clear-cut decisions based upon logic as well as instinct. In turn, there are many things about you that he will find absolutely fascinating.

To him you are creative, mystical, and fascinating, and he'll want to learn more about the magic that lies beneath the surface. Don't ever put yourself down when you're around him, though. He'll want you to have total confidence in your abilities.

He sees you as his long-lost sibling, who revels in all the parts of life that he rarely has time to examine. You see him as a solid friend, who can give you the window on a whole other world where people play games involving power and domination of some kind. Still, he will always protect you. The Capricorn Guy is traditional and loyal on the outside, but very sexy and radical on the inside. You can have fun, yet make him feel safe, too, by keeping all his little secrets!

KEEP YOUR CAPRICORN GUY!

Keeping your Capricorn Guy might not be so easy. A lot will depend on how well you can adapt to following his lead. Although he's not really a male chauvinist, he is a traditionalist. He will appreciate you and your individuality, but when it comes to living with him day to day, he'll insist on playing Tarzan to your Jane.

Be prepared to keep a comfortable home for him to come back to after long hours at the office. Even if you've had just as hard a day as he did, you'll be better off talking to a friend or colleague about it, at least until your Capricorn Guy has had time to wind down. Then, he'll be a sympathetic, loving listener, with plenty of kinky ideas about how to get you to forget all your troubles—in bed with him!

The task of keeping this lovable yet cantankerous guy in your life gets easier once you understand how your sign works with his personality. He'll appreciate it when you show proof that you're trying to please him, so read on to find out how!

Aries

You and your Capricorn Guy will get used to the game of give and take that goes on between you. It'll be fun to discover you've finally found a guy who's not afraid to take charge and hold up his end of the relationship. Keep this good thing going by realizing when it's time to simply sit back, relax, and let him give you pleasure.

When it's his turn to let you turn him on, start by hitting on some of his most sensitive body parts. His knees, particularly the area behind the leg, will be exceptionally sensitive. Your fingers or an artfully placed tongue on that area of his body will set him off and make him yours for as long as you want him!

Around the house, it might be a challenge for the two of you to decide who will be in charge of different chores. Wisdom would dictate that you do most of the things that require a lot of physical energy, while he takes on the things that require patience and perseverance.

Security, love, and the freedom to be yourself are precious gifts, and your Capricorn Guy will lovingly give them to you.

Taurus

You and your Capricorn Guy are both attracted to earth tones and practical, yet elegant furnishings—and of course, each other. That bedroom of yours is bound to get plenty of use! As he goes through every inch of your body, he'll find what a treasure of erotic response is possible from making contact with your neck, using his lips or his fingertips. Pleasing your Capricorn Guy isn't all that complicated: be more adventurous, try new techniques, and he'll keep coming back for more.

When you're in the bedroom to clean rather than make love, the two of you will have little problem agreeing on one thing—you don't like doing housekeeping! If your finances don't allow for outside help, simply schedule chores and assign specific responsibilities. Neither one of you is likely to fall down on the job.

Never let yourselves get into a rut. Travel could be one way to force you out of whatever stalled routine you might make for yourselves. Make every effort to keep your relationship more than just alive and well. He'll want to know that being with you is helping both of you—and the people around you—to thrive.

Gemini

You and your Capricorn Guy have a lot to learn from one another, and as long as you both keep an open mind, you'll build a relationship most people will envy. It's great to find someone who can appreciate you for your talents, while willingly teaching you how to constantly improve upon them.

Physically, keep him interested in you by making him rise to new challenges. Tell *him* how you want him to please you, and then turn around and do what you know will make him the happiest. And yes, you *can* get kinky! Your Capricorn Guy doesn't even know what sexual inhibition *is*!

There's no way around the fact that you're going to have to be very careful about your flirty ways. Capricorn demands total loyalty and can become deeply wounded if you don't give it to him. Let him know he's always occupying an important part of your overactive mind.

Your quick wit and his emotional distance will make this a challenging effort. To stay together, the two of you will have to remain vigilant and conscious of who you are and what wonderful things you bring to the relationship. Even when he's not easy to love, you'll probably choose to stick around. You wouldn't want to live without all those hot, sexy nights of passion, would you?

Cancer

Your Capricorn Guy will be totally in love with you because your desire to please him is so obvious. He will want to take care of your needs, too, which will touch your favorite button: security!

Although he's more reserved in public than you are, the two of you will have a hard time keeping your hands off one another when you're alone. Don't worry, though: he'll want to show you respect and care above all else, and in most cases will be perfectly well behaved.

The two of you will work out domestic matters without much fuss and bother because your respective strengths and weaknesses will be apparent. Ask yourself if you'd *really* want your Capricorn Guy to come home and try to tell you how to cook. Probably not, right?

The way to keep your relationship going is to continue to provide a home that exudes nurturing and nesting. Your Capricorn Guy is the kind of mate who will want to make wonderful family memories with you well into your golden years.

Leo

You and your Capricorn Guy have distinctively different ways of seeing the world, but that can make your relationship all that much more interesting. Combining his careful thought with your intense passion will allow you to work out just about any problem the world throws your way.

Your disagreements can easily be resolved in the bedroom. He is so attracted to you that all you need is the right place and the right time, and he'll soothe your inner, savage beast! Your job? Just let him do it.

You are not one who likes to get her hands dirty, and he is far too busy outside the home to take care of much of what's inside it. If you don't have the funds for outside help, make a game out of housekeeping that both of you can win, and your house will be neat, tidy, and filled with love.

The best way to keep your relationship safe and sound is to respect his opinions and defer to some of his ideas even when yours seem better. There really is no limit to what he'll do for you, so give in and let the pampering begin!

Virgo

If you want to keep your Capricorn Guy around, avoid reminding him when he falls short of perfection. There will always be lots to discuss, but try not to talk too much, even when you're saying something kind and supportive. He's much more into private, nonverbal expression of affection, and that's not going to change even now that you're a committed couple.

Stay on your toes in bed if you expect your Capricorn Guy to remain impressed by your knowledge and abilities. Throw in some interesting props, sex toys, or costumes that prove you want to be as appealing as you possibly can be for your man. He'll respond by sending you on deep and saucy orgasmic journeys.

Around the house, your standards for cleanliness will be far higher than his. Whether he's a CEO in the real world or not, he's going to be the king of your castle, and the king does not necessarily clean. Thankfully, he'll probably earn enough money to pay for a cleaning professional who's even more meticulous than you.

Your relationship with your Capricorn Guy won't take a lot of work, so just be extra vigilant about making him feel important and enjoy his support, comfort, and love.

Libra

Your Capricorn Guy won't deliberate much when he decides to make a commitment to your relationship. He knows what he wants, and that would be *you*. Don't keep asking him to validate your beauty or your desirability, and never waver in your love for him, or yourself.

You need to bring your relationship into the bedroom regularly, much as a car needs to go into the shop for regular maintenance. He'll tell you what he needs and wants at any given time, and will expect you to do the same. Use nonverbal means to show him what it takes to spark fireworks all over your body.

Your Capricorn Guy will allow you to take the reins when it comes to decorating the home, but let him have some say in it. Chores will have to be divided, and he'll do his part as long as you do yours. Procrastination is not in your Capricorn Guy's vocabulary, so don't shirk your duties!

Always be willing to work with your Capricorn Guy. Remember that, although he will primarily want to be the boss, he will still look to you for opinions, so bask in the comforts of a wonderfully beautiful, secure, and happy life with your Capricorn Guy!

Scorpio

The best way to keep your Capricorn Guy is to stop talking and start doing. Your sex life is very important, of course, but so is the practice of simply going places together and having a few laughs together. You'll have many common turn-ons, both in and out of the bedroom.

Sex is the underlying glue that keeps the two of you coming back for more, to be sure, and your Capricorn Guy has a lot to offer in bed. He'll insist on being the dominant force in this part of your relationship, so let yourself be chased before you reveal ways to reach orgasm he may have never dreamed about, until he met you!

You can both be territorial, so allocate some space around the home so you can each create a corner that is exclusively yours. He's not about to abide by bold colors, and you'll never throw away your deep purple curtains, will you?

Compromise is always going to be the thing you find yourself working on with your Capricorn Guy. Work with him, and in turn, he'll do what it takes to make you happy. Why? Because he's so proud to have another overachieving, ambitious person like you by his side.

Sagittarius

You'll love the way your Capricorn Guy is there when you need him, yet lets you set out on your own. Keep communication channels open, though, so you can keep the mutual trust you need to sustain your relationship.

In bed, you won't have any problem keeping up with your Capricorn Guy. In fact, he might be one of the few who has the kind of stamina that you do. As time goes by, you'll discover there's way more to him than the action between the sheets. In fact, you'll find him to be an excellent travel companion, too! The idea of being in strange and exotic places is enough to excite you, and he'll adore incorporating sex techniques from different cultures into your between-the-sheets routine.

Keeping the house clean isn't something you do naturally, but he will insist on things being in order. Before your domestic chores become a source of contention, hire someone to help you do the dirty work. You and your Capricorn Guy will stay close by honoring your individuality. Work with the friction, but don't force yourselves to fit into this partnership. Commit yourselves and trust in your solid relationship, and love will produce the tolerance and patience you'll need to stick together.

Capricorn

Carrying on a long-term relationship with someone who's *almost* exactly like you can work, as long as you both remain emotionally detached enough to honestly assess your similarities and differences. Although you're essentially the same, you will need to honor your individual needs and talents.

Sex is a cornerstone of your relationship, so don't let your busy schedules get in the way of your intimate life. Take turns bringing one another to orgasm, or engage in role-play that's as interesting as it is titillating.

Be fair about dividing household chores. Work out a schedule that's efficient and effective. You're both so reliable, it's hard to imagine how you'd ever be caught with your house in a mess!

Respect, not competition, is a good way to approach the task of relating to your Capricorn Guy. If he's really a better negotiator than you, will it be worth it to argue about that? When you're both thoroughly indulged in satisfying your sensual desires, those tiny concessions will become far easier to tolerate.

Aquarius

While your Capricorn Guy is fixed on individual achievement, you want to get people to work together for the good of everyone involved. Together, you can work to make the world better and secure a viable place in the world for you both.

During sex, let yourself go more than you usually do, and don't be shy. To your Capricorn Guy, what happens between the sheets stays there! Before long, you'll find that indulging him—and letting him please you—isn't such a bad way to spend an evening, or even a whole weekend!

Housekeeping isn't a big priority for either of you. Your Capricorn Guy might not always do what he promises, but he'll call you to the carpet if you happen to fail at meeting his expectations of you. No, it isn't fair, but that is why it's important to build up enough material wealth to afford household help when you need it.

Let go of your need to always be "right," and forget about converting him to your way of thinking. He'll learn to care more about the impact of his ideas from your example, and you'll absorb habits from him that balance your life's serious tasks with lots of steamy sex and sweet romance.

Pisces

Your Capricorn Guy isn't going to take the time to wonder what you're thinking or feeling. While he'll exhort you to grow a thicker skin, he'll also comfort you by showing you how to avoid being hurt or mishandled in the future. All he wants from you is a sympathetic ear and a warm, gentle set of arms for him to fall into when he needs a rest from the daily grind.

Your Capricorn Guy has a high sensitivity to physical sensuality, but he'll need a few lessons from you in the area of intuitively knowing what feels best and when. Be aware of your basic essence and his, and your relationship will work. He isn't without emotion—he just doesn't like to gush all over people. You are not incapable of logic—you simply like to explore the possibility of using imagination to solve problems.

Any time the communication breaks down, take him aside into your own special space and show him what it means to be loved. He'll reward you by shielding you from the parts of the world that can feel cruel while he treats you like the fairy-tale queen that you are.

YOUR CAPRICORN GUY AND . . .

No matter how adept you are at letting your Capricorn Guy believe he's the boss, there will be other people and situations in both your lives to deal with. Here's the run-down on what you can expect from some of the more complex interactions.

Your Female Friends

Your Capricorn Guy is very practical about everything, and that includes what you do with your female friends. This guy has absolutely no problem understanding the differences between male and female, and he probably won't want much to do with your girlfriends. He'll be very kind and polite to them, though, so you can always bring them to your place without worries.

Your Male Friends

Your Capricorn Guy is nothing if not territorial, so even if he tells you he doesn't mind your having some other men around now and again, he'll be watching really closely. He's not the type to act out on jealousy, at least. In fact, the way he'll try to make sure you're still dedicated to him, you lucky girl, might consist of even stronger, steamier sex than you're used to.

His Female Friends

Your Capricorn Guy will have a few female friends. They'll probably be people he's encountered in his business life, so he'll likely meet with them around the office. He likes to keep the personal and professional parts of his life kind of separate. Yes, he'll be looking and thinking sexy stuff, but only because he can't help himself. At the end of the evening, he'll put them out of his mind and come running home to you.

His Male Friends

Your Capricorn Guy wants to be part of the guys wherever he goes. His alpha-male personality and strong, quiet way of expressing himself will inspire other guys to look up to him. He'll be the one picking their meeting place, and that probably won't be around you.

He'll want to shelter you from the roughshod world he shares with his buddies, and keep your relationship as separate as possible.

Your Family

Your Capricorn Guy is the one your family has probably been wishing you'd bring home. The best kind of worker, he seems to have so much to offer. Also, because he's serious and stable, everyone will be assured he's going to take good care of you. He'll be very kind and respectful to them, and size them up to discern where you really came from.

His Family

Your Capricorn Guy is very devoted to family, but he is also realistic about them. If they're the kind who support him and the things he does, he'll offer them money and other kinds of help. If they're a pretty motley crew, he won't let them suck him dry, but he'll still respect them and insist on visiting them from time to time, just to prove his loyalty and integrity.

Your Pets

Your Capricorn Guy isn't so serious that he will never love your pets, but he isn't big on things that aren't really a necessity. He'll want your pets to be very well trained. There will be no dogs pawing through his briefcase or cats getting their claws anywhere near his leather shoes. Still, he'll respect the relationship you have with your animals and be kind, if not overly affectionate.

His Pets

A Capricorn Guy would take on pets only if he could identify some use for them. This can be protection, mousing, or even companionship.

You'll notice right away that he trains animals to make them work for him in some way. When he gets playful with them, though, that sweet and loving side of your Capricorn Guy shines right through.

His Potential for Success

Your Capricorn Guy has the brightest career stars of all. He works not just for money, but also for the prestige and power. Even if he's in a creative or philanthropic field, he'll still strive to reach the top of his field. He'll also be willing to share what he has, as long as you're pitching in with all you've got, whether it's in your own career or as a full-time caretaker at home.

His Role as a Father

A Capricorn Father is one of the best, because he embodies what most children need from parents. While he's not the warmest or most cuddly of daddies, he's got lots of other things kids love. He's strong, protective, impressive, and . . . strict. He lets children know where their limits are, and keeps them within those limits from a very early age. He strives to be someone they will always look up to.

CAPRICORN COMPATIBILITY

Your Sign	Compatibility Level
Aries	♈♈♈♈
Taurus	♉♉♉♉
Gemini	♊♊
Cancer	♋♋♋♋♋
Leo	♌♌
Virgo	♍♍♍♍
Libra	♎♎♎
Scorpio	♏♏
Sagittarius	♐♐♐
Capricorn	♑♑♑
Aquarius	♒♒♒
Pisces	♓

CAPRICORN SHORT-TERM PROSPECTS

Your Sign	Short-Term Prospects
Aries	♈♈♈♈
Taurus	♉♉
Gemini	♊♊
Cancer	♋♋♋♋
Leo	♌♌♌
Virgo	♍♍♍
Libra	♎♎
Scorpio	♏♏♏♏
Sagittarius	♐♐
Capricorn	♑♑♑
Aquarius	♒♒
Pisces	♓

CAPRICORN LONG-TERM PROSPECTS

Your Sign	Long-Term Prospects
Aries	♈♈♈♈
Taurus	♉♉♉
Gemini	♊♊
Cancer	♋♋♋♋♋
Leo	♌♌
Virgo	♍♍♍
Libra	♎♎
Scorpio	♏♏♏
Sagittarius	♐
Capricorn	♑♑♑
Aquarius	♒♒♒
Pisces	♓

CHAPTER 11

Aquarius (January 20–February 19)

YOUR MISSION: Become His Bestie

Aquarius Potential Pluses	Aquarius Potential Minuses
• Original	• Insensitivity
• Intelligent	• Coldness
• Open-minded	• Eccentricity
• Unbiased	• Stubbornness
• Interesting	• Iconoclastic
• Technically savvy	• Distracted
• Ground-breaking	• Disconnected
• Compassionate	• Unemotional
• Ambitious	• Forgetful
• Visionary	• Didactic

WHAT THE AQUARIUS GUY HAS TO GIVE . . .

The Aquarius Guy is a universe unto himself. He's independent, strong, and committed to his causes. He always tries to be different from everyone else. It's not impossible for him to be a "normal" partner in a relationship, but he will struggle against convention every step of the way. His symbol, the Water Bearer, is all about enlightenment. He pours the water of knowledge freely, hoping to elevate the masses to a more conscious, aware, hip, and activist vision of the world.

The Aquarius Guy is cool and detached, but he can still make a good partner. He won't seem to be overly affectionate, but you might be surprised by how much your approval (of everything he says, does, wears, and likes) means to him. He really wants you to be his best friend!

His determination and stubbornness come from Saturn, the planet that rules his sign. Detachment, cool logic, and rational thinking are the gifts this planet gives him. In love, he rarely lets his heart rule his head, so you have a bit of work to do! The trick is getting to his soul by jumping on his bandwagon.

As a Date:

His aloof manner and seeming detachment from what everyone else is doing set the Aquarius Guy apart from the pack. When he notices you, it will be because you have a unique look or a way about you that lets him know you believe in him and the things he holds dear to his heart.

Your first date with the Aquarius Guy will probably be set in a place where you can hear one another talk, so he can get a read on you. If he says he will call, but doesn't do it when you thought he would, don't panic. Chances are he was just distracted, or he could be too busy to go out with you at the moment.

Don't put pressure or make demands on him, and don't criticize if he wears mismatched socks or refuses to use an umbrella. This guy is completely unique and will pack up his water jug and take it elsewhere if you give any hint or suggestion that he should conform. Let him be who he is!

As a Sex Partner:

There's no doubt about it: the Aquarius Guy loves to have sex! He'll pull out all the stops to woo and seduce you. Suggestive music, gadgets that make disrobing and climbing into bed ultraconvenient: everything you might ask for—from protection to lubrication—will be on hand, and he won't stop until you say "yes" and mean it! He will want to be the best lover you've ever had and ask you what you want in the same casual way he'd enquire about your favorite music. He'll totally want to know how he can make a great impression on you, because despite his staunch quirkiness, he deeply wants to be loved.

When he has an orgasm, he might not really want you to know. It will be pretty obvious, of course, but he'll keep trying to make you pop at least five or six more times. He's going for *rave* reviews when you talk to your gal pals the morning after!

As a Domestic Partner:

The Aquarius Guy is not terribly fussy about keeping everything in its place, but he'll buy gadgets that are designed to assist him in organizing his belongings. If his place is a little disheveled, yet kind of tidy, he could be the kind of Aquarius Guy who actually knows how to clean and do laundry. If the place is neat as a pin, suspect the presence of housekeeping help.

The Aquarius Guy is anything but a chauvinist, but he can also be unreasonably demanding when it comes to sharing your funds with him. The original redistributor of wealth, the Aquarius Guy views you as an adjunct to his own philanthropic efforts. Create clear financial boundaries to avoid conflicts.

Emotionally:

Aquarius has a deep need to be loved. It's hard to recognize the frightened little boy who knows he's a little different from everybody else when he's speaking passionately about the ideals he believes in. If you're doing this right, though, you already know all this—because the two of you are best friends!

While the way he acts might lead you to believe he doesn't care what you think about him, that isn't the case at all. The Aquarius Guy will be deeply offended if you insult him or make fun of what he says and does. Although he has a good sense of humor, he'll instantly be able to tell the difference between a joke and a snarky remark. He might not demonstrate his feelings, but that doesn't mean he hasn't got deep emotions. Help him out by being extra sensitive to his need to be encouraged, appreciated, and rewarded.

When the Aquarius Guy gets mad, he may not yell or scream, but he'll detach even more profoundly than usual. Bring him back by telling him how great you think he is.

FIND YOUR AQUARIUS GUY!

The Aquarius Guy doesn't need to be hit over the head to see you're interested in him. He already assumes you are, based on his experience! To get him to select you from the variety of possibilities he feels he has, act interested in what he does, but don't come too close too soon. The quicker you can show him that you will always respect his space, the faster he will dial your digits so he can get an evening out with you.

Obviously, it's going to take some insightful tactics to read the Aquarius Guy right and get him to go along with your plan to get to know him better. Read on to see how your sign can best interact with, and attract, the coolest guy of them all!

Aries

The Aquarius Guy will find you amusing and somewhat exciting, while you find him fascinating and sexy, if a little odd. You'll be willing to overlook many of the unusual habits and ideas he might have, but he'll never stop trying to get you to look outside yourself into the world that needs help, nurturing, and good ideas. He may be slow to get involved in athletic activities, but in bed he'll definitely rise to the occasion.

When you meet him, make a comment about something he—or some other attractive person with a brilliant mind—has said. He will test you to see if you're smart enough to be his best friend. You'll know he's beginning to see you together when he starts to explain why he dresses up for Anime conventions or Renaissance Fairs.

Your sense of wonder will be something he admires and relates to. As long as you can enrich his life, he's going to keep you around. Try not to become too demanding, though. This relationship is a perpetual give-and-take until you become one another's very best friend.

Taurus

You will admire the way Aquarius gets an idea and sticks right with it. This intellectually impressive, yet elusive, guy will fascinate you. He's so brilliant that he makes you marvel about how his mind must work. His nobility and generosity will impress you, too. He'll appreciate your reliability, because he knows that it's important to be consistent, even if the only thing you can rely on about him is his unpredictability.

You might think you're too down to earth for this heady guy, but that's not so at all. He'll look at your grounded approach as one that can help anchor him enough in the real world to prevent him from floating off with one of his wild and inventive concepts, and you'll always admire his visionary outlook.

Keep listening to his ideas, but do him the favor of telling him when you think he could be deceived or cheated by the people he's dealing with. Sure, he does a lot of talking, but when he gets down to that bedroom action, he knows just how to make you feel like the earthy goddess you are.

Gemini

You will beeline your way over to the Aquarius Guy the first time you find him in the same room with you. The two of you live and thrive in the world of ideas, and he could be even more of a mental gymnast than you. You rarely have trouble starting conversations, but with the Aquarius Guy, you might have a problem ending them!

You're going to have to use more than mere talk to get the Aquarius Guy to single you out as someone who's out of the ordinary enough to be with him, though. Prove you understand complicated concepts and marvel how exciting it is to have someone who shares your interest in the intellectual. You could also say something nice about his clip-on tie or mismatched sock. Once he knows he has your acceptance, he'll be ready to take the next steps.

Your ability to adapt will be much appreciated when the Aquarius Guy starts to build a relationship with you. He can be very fixed in his ways, and because you are able to change your behavior based on circumstances, you won't mind making certain concessions and alterations to your lifestyle to mesh well into his. Follow him, and he'll take you right down the road to happiness!

Cancer

You and the Aquarius Guy share an interest in helping others, but your orientation is somewhat different. While you like to nurture and care for loved ones in your personal realm, he sees himself as (at least) the part-time savior of the world. This doesn't mean you won't get along! You'll just have to know what you can expect.

When you meet, you'll want to talk about something that illustrates that you're no mental midget. Earn his respect as an intellect, and put your playful side on display. As the Aquarius Guy seeks his best friend in his mate, you need to prove you fit the bill.

Clinginess isn't going to get you anywhere with the Aquarius Guy. If he doesn't call when he said he would, it's really okay to pick up the phone and call him. Just don't freak out on him. Your ability to sense what he's thinking and feeling will impress him far more favorably than possessiveness. Aquarius's detachment comes as much from a fear of being left alone as it does from a need for individuality and independence. Emphasize the positive, and you two could have a lot of fun together!

Leo

The Aquarius Guy is just so cool and yet, there's this regal air about him that makes you want to jump him on first sight. Your strong personality and the ability to be self-sufficient are just two of the things that make you attractive to him. He'll love it when you nurture and promote his ideas.

When you meet him, it will probably be because the two of you can't resist talking to each other. He'll find a clever way to compliment you, or you'll give him one of your million dollar smiles and his cool exterior will melt right before your eyes. Express a genuine interest in his ideas and social causes, and you'll be in!

He is going to really admire your fearlessness. Your tendency to play drama queen can get on his nerves, though, so keep that in check. When you admit that even someone as strong as you needs to lean on him from time to time, it makes him feel almost as larger than life as you are!

You will also serve as his PR agent, so he knows your dynamic personality can quickly become a big asset to you as a couple. He'll adore your sense of humor, and he'll be a sucker for your ability to relate to everyone you meet, from local royalty to the servants who have to clean up after the big party. While the two of you are quite different, you each have features that make you a totally dynamite couple.

Virgo

The Aquarius Guy's idealistic approach to life will clash with your practical way of doing things at times, but you can each offer the other a different point of view that is mutually enriching. He provides the ideas, and you organize them—but only with his consent!

You see him as someone who can offer valuable insight and service, while he views you as one *very* sexy lady! Try to live up to his impression by focusing on the pleasure principle in your relationship. He'll provide all the inspiration a girl might ever need.

While he appreciates helpful suggestions, your tendency to criticize could wear thin with him. The Aquarius Guy dreams big, and he doesn't want to be shot down before he even has a chance to explore his ideas. When you're tempted to pick out something that needs improvement, balance your criticism with a compliment of some kind. It's not easy for you to accept everything about the Aquarius Guy, but you have to at least pretend to tolerate, and even enjoy, the strange things he does!

Libra

You'll want to stand back and idolize the Aquarius Guy. The way he tries to make the world better touches you on a deep level, and you'll want to jump on his horse and ride into the sunset. He seems like the kind of guy you can say just about anything to, and you find his eccentric ways to be cute and endearing.

It could take a minute or two to turn the Aquarius Guy's head, but that won't be because he doesn't know you're gorgeous. His high level of mental activity can distract him from all else. Walk up to him, and you'll bring his train of thought to a shrieking halt.

Your combination of brains and beauty will be an immediate draw, but if there's anything about you that the Aquarius Guy won't admire, it would be your preoccupation with other people's approval. He will become a living, breathing example of someone who is a success yet doesn't care about other people's opinion at all. Most of the time, the two of you will share a likeness of mind and enough sexual heat to keep the conversation going for a mighty long time.

Scorpio

At first glance, the Aquarius Guy might not seem like your cup of tea, but ultimately, you could get totally hooked! He exudes a sense of power and mastery and has the same kind of desire for being (and being with) the best. His ideas might be unrealistic, but with a little bit of work, you theorize, they can be made into something both practical and ingenious.

You must not let the Aquarius Guy suspect you have any designs on controlling or manipulating him, so tread lightly at that first meeting! He's not gullible enough to believe you're really as shy and retiring as you try to appear. Show him who you are, and he'll come closer.

Your tenacity will be a huge turn on to the Aquarius Guy. He'll like that you hold on to your ideas and opinions. He'll enjoy the challenge of trying to get you to back down, and you'll relish dissuading him on occasion. You're impressed by his concern for other people and the state of the world; his passion for you will keep you very, very happy!

Sagittarius

The Aquarius Guy has tremendous powers of attraction, and chief among them for you is his utterly independent way of conducting his life. Here's a guy who won't be putting a leash on you or trying to get you to live in a confining cocoon with him. You sense that he has the kind of mind you could get lost in for a lifetime, and you love the way he cares so deeply about the world. His coolness and his ability to make everyone wonder what he's thinking entice you, and the little things he does to make him "eccentric" only make him more appealing.

He'll be instantly hooked on talking to you the moment he realizes there's someone who thinks at least as much and as hard as you do. You'll both strive to find solutions to problems that seem to separate people from one another. He'll love your sense of humor, as long as you don't become too boisterous or loud.

The Aquarius Guy might be somewhat put off by your restlessness and your ability to see at least two ways a problem can be solved at any given time. Although he definitely wants to find the answers, once he devises his way of taking care of an issue, he is almost impossible to dissuade. Fortunately, that encompasses the way he has chosen *you*.

Capricorn

The Aquarius Guy's way of going against the grain of society differs from your approach to life, but you'll feel strangely attracted to him. The funniest part is that you're opposite sides of the same coin. You each have a certain emotional detachment and want to stand out from the rest of the pack.

To get the attention of the Aquarius Guy, you're going to have to step out of your conventional persona long enough for him to see you have a very different side to you. A TV show or some offbeat cultural element would be a likely topic for your first conversation. Your sense of humor will surprise and impress him.

The biggest obstacle to love at first sight will be your outer image. Although you're one of the most exciting individuals anyone could know, you do have a reputation for being straight laced and uptight. Once the Aquarius Guy gets to know you better, he'll love the way you cut through the superfluous nonsense and get right to the point, especially when the two of you get up close, personal, and under the covers!

Aquarius

Whenever two Aquarius people are in the same room, they illustrate how hard it is to say what a "typical" specimen of their sign would be like. Like the fascinating Aquarius Guy, you will say and do things that make people wonder what planet you're on, all for the purpose of being different from everyone else. This could be why you and the guy you like share this unique and visionary sign. No one else understands or gets what you're talking about in quite the same way.

To get him interested, you'll have to show him how willing you are to be his friend to begin with. He might wonder what you see in him, and yet he'll play a rather rough game of hard to get. Tell him exactly what you think. He'll value honesty more than anything.

Oddly enough, the one thing he is likely to have a problem with will be *your* aloofness. Although he's the same way, he'll want you to show your warmth and affection more than you might be automatically inclined to do. Keep trying. He'll quickly come to love your original way of doting on him.

Pisces

For you, going out with the Aquarius Guy is a bit like diving into the deep end of the pool before you've learned how to swim. This emotionally aloof guy can be interesting and irresistible to you, nonetheless! You admire the way he seems totally independent and self-sufficient, and you want to be more like him, if you can.

To impress the Aquarius Guy, you'll have to prove that you won't depend on him for anything. Although he will care for you and even pamper you at times, he won't want you to drain his energy. You do share compassion and a desire to care for the entire world, so make sure you point this out at your first meeting. He'll try to pose and posture himself to appear to be your superior, but in truth, you have some attributes that he could learn a lot from too.

Even at your spaciest, you always process feelings and turn them into profound thoughts. Show him how valuable the emotional perspective can be, even if he laughs it off. Remember: there are no life preservers when you jump into the pool of love with the Aquarius Guy.

Keep Your Aquarius Guy!

There will be days when you want to work hard to keep your Aquarius Guy, and times when you wonder why you keep trying! His avoidance of being "tied down" is one obstacle; trying to understand him in all his unpredictability is another. Still, with all his faults, he *can* be adorable. Your ability to let him be who he is will be the factor that keeps you together. Can you do it? Sure—anyone can, with the right strategy!

As a rule, keeping your Aquarius Guy interested is a matter of letting him know you're willing to be his best buddy. This means that you will accept his oddities and embrace his causes as though they are your own. You may not spend each and every minute of your lives together, but having your separate experiences will make your conversations even more lively and filled with laughter than you thought they would be!

How well can you achieve the status of "bestie" with your Aquarius Guy? Use the magic action of your sign to interact with Aquarius in a way that keeps the friendship going and the passion alive.

Aries

Learning to balance your own need for physical activity with his tendency to live the life of the mind will bring good things to both of you. You'll have to work on your listening skills to keep up with the topics he wants to discuss, and he'll have to learn your limits when it comes to staying in any one place for too long.

Your sex life will be one of the best things about your relationship. Of course, you'll be undeniably attracted to one another, but you'll be more excited about the physicality of your relationship than he will. While you never mind being the one to get things started, you might have to let him know when you need him to pay more attention to what you need.

At home, you won't see the sense in his obsessive collecting, and he won't share your ruthless attitude toward discarding stuff you don't use. In his mind, there's always something he can do with almost anything! Focus more on making sure the one thing he'll always want to play with is you! Once you adopt him as your best friend for life, the happiness you're after will appear in abundance.

Taurus

What happens when you start dating your Aquarius Guy, who has as much staying power as you do, yet seems to be free to pursue all the heady ideas his mind can handle? You fall head over heels, that's what! The two of you might not seem like a match, but in truth you have more in common than your friends might believe. He helps you raise your consciousness, and you keep him tied to the earth.

Your Aquarius Guy has an extremely sexy persona, but when it gets down to the hugging and rubbing, you've got it all over him. Your sensuality is something he's going to totally admire about you, and he'll knock himself out trying to create one explosive orgasm after the other.

Household chores are not his specialty, so you will probably be the one who does most of the decorating and cleaning. He might insist on a few unusual items or a slew of electronics being on display. It certainly won't be pretty, but if you didn't have these things around, how would you know you were living with an Aquarius Guy?

Gemini

Your Aquarius Guy is really a rather perfect match for you, because you both seek lifelong friendship from a mate and are very capable of providing it for one another. He'll appreciate your ability to instantly understand what he means when he speaks, and offer you enough excitement to satisfy even overactive you.

The two of you will enjoy having sex because it's a way to express all the things you feel without using words to describe them. Set aside time for weekend getaways and times when you go off the grid together, just long enough to reconnect by making love.

Organize your household by treating it like a work project. Your Aquarius Guy's sense of fairness will never leave you holding the bag, whether it's filled with garbage or items that need to be donated to his favorite charity.

Happiness is easy to come by for you two. The only thing you might have to watch out for his fear of losing you. You have so many friends in your life, and he can feel left out unless you go out of your way to include him. Don't worry. There will always be enough space left for the two of you to be the outstanding individuals you are!

Cancer

Making a commitment to your Aquarius Guy is a very brave step for you. You are two different kinds of people and your motives will be tested here. If you're really sincere about taking care of someone, it must be because you love him for who he really is.

Show your Aquarius Guy you're willing to do what it takes, starting in the bedroom. Wait for him to come to you, and he'll shower the rewards all over your body! It can be difficult for you to trust anyone with your heart, but if you display any evidence of wariness with this guy, he will be deeply wounded. If he does withdraw from you, look into his eyes. He will see the love—and lust—you have for him, deep within your soul.

One thing you'll truly like about being with your Aquarius Guy is that he'll allow you to be the domestic goddess you are! You will teach him the lesson of consistency and care, while he teaches you to be independent and strong. Sounds like a great deal, right?

Leo

Your Aquarius Guy is a great match for you, and once you make your commitment you'll understand why that's so true. He seems to fill all of your needs, without falling helplessly at your feet. The fact he is not overly gushy is a challenge to you, but you'll work it out.

Sexually, he'll treat you like a queen! No one else seems to know how much you need to be admired without being adored. Being with your best friend this way is a refreshing, rejuvenating experience, and the two of you have a balanced way of fitting intimacy into your life without letting it get in the way of your individual responsibilities. Neither one of you is particularly fond of doing the dirty work around the house, but when it needs to be taken care of, you're usually the one to get it started, but he'll help out.

This relationship will work without too much effort, but it will become outstanding when you pay rapt attention to how you treat one another and ensure that respect and caring are always the motivation behind what you do and say.

Virgo

If you want to "tame" your Aquarius Guy, you'll have to let go of any attempt to tell him how to run his life. He'll ask for help when he wants your advice on how to organize his life, and he'll offer you an objective ear that helps you see into your day-to-day relationships.

You are a very dynamic lover, and so is your Aquarius Guy. He appreciates the way you tend to every detail of providing him with pleasure, and he has a super-human way about him that makes you awfully glad to have him in your bed. Always keep your sex life as a staple of your relationship routine!

You are definitely much more likely to take care of the house than your Aquarius Guy will be, but he can be of help nonetheless. He will be the one to remind you that you really *can* leave a dirty spoon in the sink now and then without catching some dread disease. Staying together will be easy if you remember you have a lot of gaps to bridge. You see the world in two different ways, and your posture must be that you have a lot to learn from one another.

Libra

Your friendship with your Aquarius Guy feels as natural as breathing for both of you, so even making a commitment is easy and breezy. You seem to see most things the same way, and you enjoy your conversations because they combine his scientific and social views with your aesthetic and interpersonal insights.

You might not need a lot of advice about your sex life, either! The two of you are both capable of inventing new ways to show your love and devotion without the use of words. You may have to provide more of the mood-setting elements to the equation, though, with your artful seduction.

Make an effort to keep your abode looking as harmonious on the surface as your love for one another is! You take the chores that require negotiating skills and an artful hand, while he'll be much better at tasks that require technical know-how and group cooperation.

Love like the one you can cultivate with Aquarius doesn't come along every day! You'll stay together in peace and harmony as long as you cherish your bond.

Scorpio

Your Aquarius Guy is a great match for you, mainly because he's a strong enough individual to avoid being crushed by your dominant personality. He'll also totally understand why you want to do everything possible to make it work perfectly.

Your sexuality will be a revelation to your Aquarius Guy, but he'll have no problem getting used to it!

You'll be the one to tend to details around the house, because . . . well, you're good at it! While your Aquarius Guy will have terrific ideas about where to put things or how to streamline certain procedures, he's not into the hands-on parts of housework.

Keep your love alive with as much communication as possible. You need him to be your "rock," and he looks up to you for your ability to stand up for yourself. There will be times when he gets lost in the worries of the world. That'll be your cue to take him aside, look into his eyes, and insist you make wild, passionate love until he can no longer tell where he ends and you begin.

Sagittarius

You and your Aquarius Guy make a very cute couple, because you're both filled with ideas and dreams that truly could make the world a better place. This is a great place for you to start, but to keep your commitment from wavering, you'll have to get the right combination of freedom and support.

Your ability to connect sexually will only add to your happiness. Although he won't be as demonstrative as you are, he'll be very artful about the way he pleases you. You can make him feel good by slowing down to appreciate all the beautiful things about his body.

You're going to have to pay more attention to the way you keep your house because your Aquarius Guy isn't going to love living in a mess, no matter how "organized" you insist it is! Let him teach you about following through, even with the laundry and scrubbing the bathroom.

The love that flows with such ease between you will flourish when you keep the communication going. Even though you'll have separate, busy lives, the conversations you have together will be a great reason to reserve time for just the two of you.

Capricorn

You and your Aquarius Guy can create an amazingly peaceful life together, but you'll both need to make a few concessions. You'll see why this is necessary, particularly when you want to stick with traditions, and he can't wait to rebel against them.

Settle your disputes in the bedroom. You'll be far more willing to accept your Aquarius Guy's need to be a little more childish and playful when he joins in on those sex games you love so much. In turn, he'll gladly behave when you show him who's boss.

If you think you can depend on your Aquarius Guy to keep the household in a state of order, you'll need to adjust your expectations. He's not a slob, but he's no domestic miracle worker either. You'll have to take charge of the home improvement projects, but you can delegate the parts that require scientific or technical genius to him.

Acknowledging who you each are is the key to keeping yourselves content in this relationship. Each of you could use a few lessons in expressing affection. Always be thoughtful of each other, and give hugs and kisses even when you don't think they're really needed.

Aquarius

You might not have thought there could possibly be anyone else as independent and original as you, but then you met your Aquarius Guy! The two of you will have more interesting conversations in one week than most other people have in their entire lives.

Because neither of you likes to be the first one to take your intense mental and spiritual connection to the physical level, you might have to work extra hard to reserve that special kind of time to be together. You can do it!

Your home will be interesting to visit, but it won't be conventional. The two of you would rather have an ultramodern, simply decorated home than a soft, cushy, and traditional one. Although neither of you is so averse to housework that you won't do it, you surely don't view cleaning as a therapeutic act.

Affection is the thing that will keep your relationship together. You might think you don't need all that gushy stuff going on between the two of you, but when you're on the receiving end of it, no one will hear you complain. Your two bodies will gleefully become a single source of love.

Pisces

You should be congratulated for having the courage to get close to your Aquarius Guy, and now you might wish you'd met him years before! It's great if you're learning how to ask for what you want from him, as you perceive he needs more of your undying devotion than he dares to let on.

Sexually, the Aquarius Guy has the power to give you deep, transformative feelings that lead you to see how the two of you can create very beautiful music together. Getting his attention is easy: just look at him!

Friends and family will muse at how two people who seem to come from two different worlds can get along so well and put together a home that exudes the feeling of love. Your Aquarius Guy isn't a great housekeeper; he'll help with electronics! You'll still have to learn, because he'll teach you rather than do it for you every time.

No matter what kinds of possessions you have in your house, as long as the two of you are there, making every effort to fill one another's needs, there will be enough love for you and everyone who knocks at your door to enjoy.

YOUR AQUARIUS GUY AND . . .

The fun really gets started when you try to integrate your Aquarius Guy into the other people and things in your life. Read on to see how he'll typically react as he gets acquainted with friends, family, and pets, and what you can expect from him as a provider and parent.

Your Female Friends

Your Aquarius Guy will be tolerant and welcoming when you bring your girlfriends to your house or go out somewhere along with them. He'll engage with them and try to show off his considerably wonderful mind just to make sure they know how lucky you are, and keep reminding you of the same. You'll be very proud to show him off, too.

Your Male Friends

As long as you're not betraying any promise you might have made to him, your Aquarius Guy will be extremely tolerant of you being with other men. He has an easy time understanding that you can get into a friendship with a guy and still be in love with your Aquarius Guy at the same time. He also hopes you're just as sensitive and tolerant with him!

His Female Friends

That cool and alluring personality of his is going to draw in lots of females, and some of them will be content to be just friends. These ones you can tolerate with no problem, because he probably brings them around to meet you and get to know you better. There will be others, though, who have more amorous intentions. Hide your jealous streak! It's unlikely that your Aquarius Guy will cheat on you, so there's no reason to worry about losing him.

His Male Friends

The men your Aquarius Guy hangs with will be an interesting collection of characters. You'll enjoy meeting them and will probably see them often around your house. When they go out together, it will usually be for something that would bore you or gross you out. You'll be happy to stay behind.

Your Family

Your Aquarius Guy is always going to try to be the one who sticks out like a sore thumb at your family gatherings, for whatever reason he can invent. Unless they already have some of his same type in their ranks, your family will have difficulty embracing him. Just as you think it's hopeless, your Aquarius Guy will do something wonderful that turns him into your family's most precious gem.

His Family

Your Aquarius Guy is loyal to his family, but he'll be somewhat emotionally detached from them, too. They probably learned long ago that the way to make him come back to visit is to pretend it doesn't really matter that much to them. Always trying to be the odd one out, your Aquarius Guy pushes the envelope and irritates his kin, just to test whether what they say is true—they'll love him no matter what.

Your Pets

The nobility of animals will always attract your Aquarius Guy, and he'll take to your pets right away. In fact, during those awkward moments in the early part of your relationship, when there doesn't seem to be much to say, he'll look to your pet as a way to connect with you. He'll show you it's possible to love people (or an animal) while allowing them to be who they are.

His Pets

Your Aquarius Guy will always look for the animal that, like him, has that "something different" quality about him. Whether it's a shelter cat or a weird breed of dog, he'll want his pet to reflect his own need to stand out from the crowd. You'll enjoy seeing him with his pets, because he'll show off his quirky-yet-endearing way of connecting with them, and you'll get a glimpse of how he'll use his heart to get to you.

His Potential for Success

Your Aquarius Guy will probably make a good living in spite of himself. His skills usually skew toward science, technology, and engineering. Even artistic Aquarius Guys make money, because they have one hand in the technical side of the arts, where there's somewhat more money. The worst problem you might have is watching him give it away to causes that matter to him. Keep a close eye on your own reserves.

His Role as a Father

There's nothing like an Aquarius dad, especially for a kid who's got a penchant for the funny, the weird, and the scientific. There will be cool science experiments being carried out in your bathroom, kitchen, and microwave. As the child grows, though, your Aquarius dad might have to drop the silliness and adopt a more serious attitude so as to prepare his progeny for the realities of the world.

AQUARIUS COMPATIBILITY	
Your Sign	**Compatibility Level**
Aries	♈♈
Taurus	♉♉♉♉
Gemini	♊♊♊♊
Cancer	♋♋
Leo	♌♌♌♌♌
Virgo	♍
Libra	♎♎♎
Scorpio	♏♏♏♏
Sagittarius	♐♐
Capricorn	♑♑
Aquarius	♒♒♒
Pisces	♓

AQUARIUS SHORT-TERM PROSPECTS	
Your Sign	**Short-Term Prospects**
Aries	♈♈♈
Taurus	♉♉♉♉
Gemini	♊♊♊
Cancer	♋♋
Leo	♌♌♌♌
Virgo	♍
Libra	♎♎♎
Scorpio	♏♏♏♏
Sagittarius	♐♐
Capricorn	♑♑♑
Aquarius	♒♒
Pisces	♓

AQUARIUS LONG-TERM PROSPECTS	
Your Sign	**Long-Term Prospects**
Aries	♈♈♈
Taurus	♉♉♉♉
Gemini	♊♊♊♊
Cancer	♋
Leo	♌♌♌♌♌
Virgo	♍♍
Libra	♎♎♎
Scorpio	♏♏♏♏
Sagittarius	♐♐
Capricorn	♑♑
Aquarius	♒♒♒
Pisces	♓

CHAPTER 12

Pisces (February 21–March 20)

YOUR MISSION: Tread Softly and Be Patient

Pisces Potential Pluses

- Sensitive
- Caring
- Imaginative
- Sympathetic
- Nurturing
- Attentive
- Artistic
- Kind
- Emotionally open
- Intellectually creative

Pisces Potential Minuses

- Spaced-out
- Hypersensitive
- Unstable
- Lost in fantasy world
- Unreliable
- Late
- Unambitious
- Imprecise
- Distractable
- Disorganized

WHAT THE PISCES GUY HAS TO GIVE . . .

This man is soulful, cute, and gives you adoring looks that make you feel like the luckiest woman in the universe. A Pisces seems to be with you 150 percent while you're together, but in truth he probably never knows what he really wants. Like the two fish that comprise his symbol, just as you think you've got him by the tail, he'll swim away! It is possible to harness the compassion and caring this man feels for the world and have him direct it toward you and your relationship, but you'll need to be patient.

The Pisces Guy isn't as easy to "get" as he seems. He picks up the mood and the opinions of the people he's around so he can change from day to day based on who he's been spending the most time with. Understand first that this man has a deep, genuine love for the world, especially people who need to be taken care of. His ruling planet, Jupiter, bestows a generosity that's refreshingly uncommon. The more you can see the world through his compassionate eyes, he'll see you're loving and wonderful, too.

Trust is a huge deal to the Pisces Guy. Because he goes through life assuming most people are nice, good, and want to do the best things for him, he often gets disappointed. He might go back and forth several times before deciding you're the "one," and even after that happens you're still going to have to prove you can be trusted before he'll settle in, get comfortable, and open like the flower of love that he is.

As a Date:

The Pisces Guy is quiet and unassuming, and once you meet him you'll see that he is very talented at picking up the mood of the room, and finding the best way to blend in. His emotions run very deeply, and he will be touched by your attention.

A fun date with Pisces will probably involve some sort of escape into a world beyond the mundane. The movies would be a good place to start, but because Pisces appreciates all forms of imagination, it could also be a night at the theater, a rock concert, or even a puppet show!

You might have to work really hard to let the Pisces Guy know you want him. Though he has some pride in his winning qualities he may find it hard to believe you'd really want to be with him!

Pisces has a sensitivity that you'll feel from the first time you see him. He is the kind of guy you want to take charge of, and showing you could do that will encourage him. He's pretty mushy-gushy in public, so if you blush when you get kissed or felt in public, don't let it show.

If he can't let you know how he feels about you, he'll be terribly hurt and unfulfilled. This is the down side of his sensitivity. You can hurt his feelings by looking in the wrong direction at the right moment. No one else has as much ability to communicate on the deepest, feeling levels than the adorably, if seemingly helpless, Pisces Guy!

As a Sex Partner:

If you want the kind of partner who looks lovingly into your eyes while the two of you have passionate sex, this is your man. The Pisces Guy is very capable of enjoying the physical angle of intercourse, but for him to really participate in it, there has to be an extremely strong emotional or spiritual component. Still, you can't automatically assume you're a "couple" just because you've been to bed together. Pisces will wait as long as possible before he makes a final commitment to be yours alone.

Get to Pisces through his most sensitive body part: the feet. If you're not a Pisces, that might not sound like the sexiest place to start, but it works. When your Pisces Guy has an orgasm, you may think he's been taken over by some demon—or angel. He'll thank you, several deities, his mom, and just about anyone else while in a state of pure bliss. And he'll reciprocate, often!

As a Domestic Partner:

Your Pisces Guy could be so detached from reality that he has no clue about how to cook, wash clothes, or clean up after himself. Or, he might hate to see you do these things. You might want to stop him at the point where he starts to iron your clothes for you every morning, but if he enjoys it, who are you to say he should stop?

Sometimes your Pisces Guy seems to be more concerned about people outside your relationship, including the world at large. Watching him cry over the images of children on the TV while you've got a high fever could get a little bit frustrating. Just remind him, gently, that you still need a glass of water, and he'll get it!

Emotionally:

When you get up close and personal with the Pisces Guy, you soon realize you're going to have to be "the strong one" in the relationship. He might try to put up a front that displays something resembling a stiff upper lip, but he's really quite the softie, emotionally speaking.

Part of the reason he takes so long to make a commitment is the extreme level of trust he needs to build up before he knows he will be safe with you. When (not "if") you hurt your Pisces Guy's feelings, you'll know right away, because he's likely to either turn away or cry right in your face. The problem is, you'll never know *when* he'll get deeply wounded. You certainly don't want to ever let him think you're not there for him, but that's not always possible.

The storm created by a Pisces Guy's emotional upset can be frightening, but lucky for you, it's easy enough to calm him down. Simply wrap your arms around him, apologize if you have to, and hold him until he returns to a less volatile state. He'll thank you for being there for him, profusely.

FIND YOUR PISCES GUY!

The Pisces Guy will take his time at showing he knows you're interested in him. Much of the communication between you will be without words. Be conscious of your body language, and project the image of being captivated without taking on the posture of a captor. He'll be attracted by your interest in him but wary if you get too lustful or lascivious at first sight. Save the sexy stuff for later. In the beginning, be a shining example of openness, honesty, and trustworthiness.

The way your sign interacts with Pisces will tell you more about how to find your way into his heart. Keep reading for tips that get you there faster than you thought possible.

Aries

Tread softly, because a strong, direct manner is probably going to scare the Pisces Guy off. You will have to practice almost constant restraint to ratchet down the level of your inner intensity, and this is especially important when you're dealing with such a sensitive person. He'll know you want to do fabulously naughty things to his body, but he's going to wait until he's ready to let you get anywhere near him.

Chill and be still before you make your initial approach. The Pisces Guy will want you to stand back and let him show you what his world is all about before you dive in to become a part of it. Later, as he comes to trust you, he'll look to you for courage and leadership.

A friendly call or flirty e-mail will keep you in his mind when he gets overwhelmed and slightly forgetful. Be sympathetic with him so the two of you can both be the "baby" in your relationship.

Taurus

You'll instantly like the way the Pisces Guy seems to exist in his own little world of magic and fantasy. He will give you a way of escaping your own rut, where everything is geared toward acquiring and keeping the trappings of safety and security. You will love his sensitivity, and he'll see right away that underneath your earnest, earthy manner, you have a very good heart.

You won't have any trouble approaching him, because he'll detect your warmth so quickly. Don't be worried if he doesn't call you right away after you meet, though. You might need to remind him you agreed to meet again, but a calm and friendly call will do.

There are lots of things the Pisces Guy will love about you. He'll detect immediately that you have the ability (if not the desire) to take care of all the things he needs. This guy might not notice, at the same time, that you have some basic maintenance needs, too. Don't be insulted. Eventually, his sensitivity will kick in, and once he gets on your "frequency," he'll pick up the signals that you're sending out.

Gemini

There might be a few things that you and the Pisces Guy won't agree on, but for the most part it's pretty easy for the two of you to get along. Pisces will keep you comfortable by offering the freedom you need to preserve your individuality. He'll see the idea of commitment to be a process, a very slow one, so you won't be so worried about being boxed in or smothered by this relationship.

To get started, all you really need to do is be friendly and talk. Pisces will notice your charms almost instantly, and when you speak he will always eagerly listen! Remember to ask him a few questions, too, so he has concrete evidence that you're as capable of being as caring a partner as he is.

He'll look to you to bring him out and into the world, and your friends will be impressed by his creativity. You'll love showing off how well he and you get along. Together, you create a combination of mental and emotional sensibility that makes you a great team.

Cancer

The Pisces Guy and you will get along right away, because he might be one of the few people you meet who's equipped with the same kind of emotional intelligence you have. You are always hoping to have someone to take care of, and this guy, with his less-than-steady way of functioning in the real world, will fit the bill perfectly.

Introduce yourself to him by showing him right away that you can pick up on his feelings. He'll be impressed, if a little bit daunted, at how quickly you could get a read on him. Try to reassure him that you have nothing but the best of intentions.

Do your best not to get jealous or possessive if he talks about or shows his affection for people you don't really know. He still loves you! It's just that his heart, really and truly, is large enough to fit in a whole world of affection. He will seem to have a lot of people in his life who are "users." While you'll want to protect him as much as possible, he won't want you to intrude every time. Make it clear that certain comments come out of caring rather than clinginess and possessiveness.

Leo

You and the Pisces Guy will have to work hard to keep your relationship afloat, but that doesn't mean you won't be intensely attracted to one another. Yor sign is fiery and his is watery, but if you work this right, you could wind up making a very steamy couple!

When you first meet, you'll want to start with nonverbal cues that let him know you could be interested. Don't scare him off by being brash or loud or giving him an inkling that you might laugh at him. He'll respond best if you ask him questions. Make that extra effort to listen to, and hear, his answers. He has a lot to say, but he will open up only slowly. He will give you the kinds of compliments you like to get, but you'll have to understand he can't ever be totally dedicated to giving you everything you want at the exact moment you ask for it.

He will deeply admire your integrity and appreciate the way you strive to bring out the best in him. You share a universal caring for humanity that will keep your love alive.

Virgo

You and the Pisces Guy fit so well together because you're so different! He is a bit of a fuzzy thinker, with an emphasis on instincts and emotions, while you can analyze your way around almost any problem, and believe in the power of thinking. He wants someone to take care of him, and you see him as your personal work in progress.

To meet a Pisces Guy, you'll have to look outside of your usual circle of friends and colleagues. Look for him in places where imagination rules, such as a movie theater, dance club, or theater company. When you approach him, be sure to let him know how much you admire him for what he does, and ask him to teach you how to be more creative.

It takes a very strong ego to realize that, when you point out someone's mistakes or intrinsic flaws, you only want to help them be better than they already are. Pisces doesn't come with a very strong sense of self-esteem, so when you help him along, do it in as nurturing and supportive a way as possible, and he'll appreciate the way you cut down on the chaos and offer a steady stream of love.

Libra

The Pisces Guy totally fascinates you because there are so many things about you two that seem to run in parallel. You both love the arts and believe that the world of beauty should always intersect with what you see on earth. You are also both pure, peaceful souls.

When you meet the Pisces Guy, it will probably be because you see him noticing some work of art or a beautiful object at the same time you do. A silent smile between you will say almost everything there is to say about your connection. If you repair to a place where you can possibly indulge in a glass of wine or a cup of coffee and more conversation, you'll swear you've come across someone who could become your soul mate.

No relationship is idyllic, and you will discover early on that there are certain things that set you and the Pisces Guy apart. One of them might be your indecisiveness. It's not that he's such a great decision maker! Still, one of you will have to make a choice so you can move forward. If you can do that, a fulfilling life of love and beauty lies ahead!

Scorpio

You and the Pisces Guy get what the other is about because you share a deeply emotional way of perceiving the world and have the desire to build a relationship that allows you to relate totally on the soul level. You'll have an instant attraction to one another as friends and can easily let this grow into an even more profoundly loving connection.

When you meet Pisces, the two of you will feel as though you've known one another for ages. Not only will he share your "touchy-feely" way of interacting with people, but he'll also be an exquisite listener. No question: your spiritual and social connection will always be solid. If you want to turn him on, though, you're going to have to hold back on any impulse to act possessive or domineering.

Pisces will admire your strength, even if he remains a little bit afraid of it. After all, he wonders if you'll ever turn your aggressive behavior patterns in his direction. Try to allay his fears by advocating for him whenever you can, and giving him the kind of unconditional love he so willingly offers to you.

Sagittarius

You might think two people couldn't be more different, but you and the Pisces Guy will find you actually have a whole lot in common. Just for starters: the two of you share a ruling planet, Jupiter. You display this huge planet's jovial side, while the Pisces Guy will display the universal love Jupiter is also known for.

Tone it down when you first meet the Pisces Guy. Your cheerfulness will be more than welcome, but if you come on as being too strong or boisterous, this could put him off. At least he'll feel as though he can really trust you, right from the get-go, so he'll open up to you far more easily than usual.

The Pisces Guy will love your generous spirit and truly appreciate your sense of humor. You can joke with him and feel safe that he won't play stupid practical jokes on you. In fact, he'll commiserate about what it's like to be a wide-open person, and how people often take advantage of your good nature. The friendship and affinity the two of you feel will keep the fire of passion burning. All you really have to do is sit back and enjoy the ride.

Capricorn

The Pisces Guy is sweet, kind, and generous but nowhere near as street smart as you are! Your ruling planet, Saturn, gives you the ability to structure and organize things. The Pisces Guy's affinity toward Jupiter gives him a spirit that can be too generous. He may give things away even before he's had time to enjoy them.

When you first meet, the attraction could crop up because you're intrigued about what this interesting-looking guy is thinking. Lost in imagination and bent toward the creative and artistic, he's rarely terribly logical about anything. Talk more about the lighter side of life, and the two of you will relate a lot more easily.

Your concrete, black-and-white way of thinking might not appeal to the Pisces Guy. He could feel restricted and constrained by your insistence on following tradition and putting forth the appearance of being straight laced with a de-emphasis on imagination. On the other hand, because he really does need you to watch over him, he'll adore the way you take care of business. If you can deal with a little bit of role-reversal, this relationship will be warm and rewarding.

Aquarius

You and the Pisces Guy are pretty likely to meet because you'll be found in the part of the room that's away from the fray and the noise. You both enjoy being set apart from the crowd, and this alone is enough to attract you to one another. You'll also be very taken by his ability to transcend reality and get carried off into the realm of ideas and imagination with you.

When you approach him, show him your open-minded side. It isn't easy for this person to talk to strangers, because he fears being judged by people who don't understand him. Can you relate to that? Thought so.

You'll have to go slowly as you get closer to the Pisces Guy. He won't be quite sure about you, because he'll notice how you don't seem to work with feelings the same way he does. Make it clear that the fact you don't break into tears at the drop of the hat doesn't prove you don't care about him, humanity, or anything else. If each of you takes a little of what the other has, you both can become warm and loving as well as stable, and have a magnificent time together.

Pisces

What more could you ask for than to meet someone who, finally, understands you? The Pisces Guy will be all that and more. If you work hard at building your relationship, you could easily become the kind of couple that finishes one another's sentences and start to look like one another a few years into your blissful togetherness.

The smiles you exchange after that are sure to lead to a conversation. The most difficult part is likely to be keeping your hands off each other! The attraction between two Pisces people really is that strong. After all, the symbol of your sign is two fishes swimming together, in an eternal circle.

The one downside of the two of you being together is you won't have many forces working upon you that might ease your less-than-organized outlook on life. You can't help being just as befuddled as he is; but he could get frustrated when you don't suddenly become the mature guide he needs. Still, by going along your merry way, swimming together, chasing each other around the circle, you will feel you have found your soul mate, and will have no desire to be with or around anybody else.

KEEP YOUR PISCES GUY!

Your Pisces Guy can be as slippery as the fish that's part of his symbol. He spends such a lot of time inside his mind, exploring his imagination and fantasizing about a world of magic, mysticism, and beauty that transcends the ordinary human experience. He also fears commitment because he is so vulnerable to being hurt.

To increase your chances of keeping your Pisces Guy happy as a clam, you'll have to allow for, and even invite, his indulgence in a fantasy world. You won't mind it when he invents wild stories while you're in the process of having sex because once Pisces gets his imagination going, you won't have to fake a thing in the way of orgasmic Nirvana. Letting him dream his way through a financial crisis, on the other hand, can be quite another thing. You may not love micromanaging his time-consuming, real-life affairs, but it's well worth the magical presence of the otherworldly Pisces Guy!

Read on to see how your sign taps into this mystical guy so you can keep your love going, glowing, and growing in years to come.

Aries

Channeling your fierce energy to calm down for your Pisces Guy will be an interesting challenge. Yet, you'll love going to adventure movies together, and he'll cheer you on toward success in the material world. Friends on the outside will wonder how you reconcile your differences, but when they see how you keep his feet on the ground and he chills you out, they'll understand.

In bed, Pisces will look to you for cues because he figures you're "hotter" than he is. In truth, he's just as skilled as you are, but he knows that when you think you're in control of your orgasms, you'll love them all the more. He might need time when it comes to his own orgasms, so be patient!

Your house will be a lot like the rest of your relationship—a mixture of seeming opposites that blends perfectly. Your taste for bright colors will break up the ennui of pastel watercolors Pisces tends to favor.

If you want to keep this relationship as happy as it felt at your first kiss, practice being gentle and loving with your Pisces Guy. He might not attempt wall climbing or bound from one tall building to the next, but in bed, if you remember to slow down, stroke him gently, and let his love for you unfold, your Pisces Guy will be the ultimate superhero.

Taurus

You and your Pisces Guy will have a lot of nice conversations. He'll broaden your view of the world and help you gain more sympathy for people. He'll also introduce you to a lot of new friends. Meanwhile, you'll help him communicate more effectively, because you won't really be able to understand him and his ethereal ideas without a clear explanation. Your friends will notice how this dynamic works, and agree that the two of you make a great couple.

Sexually, your Pisces Guy is all for long, slow sessions that bring you to crazy orgasms. When he comes, he seems to fly off to another world, only to float back to earth, more in love with you than ever.

You'll be more domestically oriented than your Pisces Guy, but he'll happily add artistic touches. You'd both rather ditch the decorating and just stay in the bedroom!

Sticking with your Pisces Guy is easy. Just allow him to be who he is. No, he isn't the typical man; but he is an extraordinary partner, lover, and friend. Maintain a spirit of mutual nurturing and tolerance, and keep reminding yourself that he has to make some concessions to coexist with you, too!

Gemini

He might never be a Master of the Universe at work but you'll admire your Pisces Guy's cool authority, especially in matters that concern intuition and creativity. He'll look to you as his "home base," even before you live together.

Your bedroom activities will be magical, as long as you can refrain from straying! Not only will he send you to another plane of pleasure, his own orgasms make you feel like a miracle worker. Don't get spooked when he looks into your eyes and reads your soul! Making love with your Pisces Guy is a mystical experience.

Your home life will be peaceful, because you won't have problems giving one another the alone time you each need so much. You'll still get to roam the world and "work the room." Make dates to watch your favorite DVDs or listen to his otherworldly music from time to time in that special space. The key to keeping your Pisces Guy happy is to pay attention to him and take consideration of his feelings at all times. He'll reward you with undying friendship and some of the most amazing sex you've ever had.

Cancer

You and Your Pisces Guy anticipate one another's needs like a pair of psychics. He'll adore the way you take care of him, and you'll appreciate it when he writes you poetry or plays you a song at the most perfect, romantic moment.

The two of you will spend hours trying to find new ways to please each other sexually. He'll read your moods and do whatever it takes to seduce you. A master of foreplay, he'll love to cuddle and coo, even when you don't have time to "go all the way."

You'll be happy to take care of most of the chores around the house, but let him participate, too. He will rarely be the guy who stands up and claims to be a man's man, but you can use your nurturing way to teach him how to pull his weight around the house.

The key to keeping your love alive is to be realistic. He might not be perfect, but he is a really wonderful partner. Don't expect him to read your mind all of the time, and he'll excuse you when you're off the mark about what he wants. Accept, embrace, and love one another.

Leo

You and your Pisces Guy won't see eye to eye on everything, but you'll still glow when you're together. You share a mutual fascination.

Your friends might wonder what brought you together, but they'll all agree that you seem a lot happier since you've been that way.

Love on the physical plane will be a highlight of your relationship. You want to be worshipped, and your Pisces Guy will want to show how much he adores you. He'll be thrilled to bring you to one orgasm after the next, and you'll be amazed at how he dives so deeply into his own climax with his mind, body, and soul.

Around the house and in life, your Pisces Guy will not fight to take charge of anything. Negotiate ways to deal with household management, and professional help might be needed to do the heavy lifting when it comes to keeping your lair looking royal.

To make this stick, always respect him and remember to appreciate the way he sensitizes you to his and others' feelings. He admires your strength more than you know, but he also has secret strategies that turn you into a helpless, purring pussycat.

Virgo

You and that sweet, gentle Pisces Guy have a lot in common, and you can achieve a near-perfect union if you're willing to put a smidgen of work into it. With your ability to tend to details, and his ability to dream, you have most of the continuum of life handled and under control.

Making time to make love is easy with him. When you're stressed and distracted, he'll listen to you talk while he massages your back and kisses you lightly on the neck. What could you have to complain about? He shows you a spiritual side to sex that makes it truly miraculous.

His housekeeping habits might be somewhat harder for you to get used to! Pisces doesn't "do" sweeping, dusting, and scrubbing with the unrelenting vigor you would like him to. The only time you *won't* mind this so much is when he strews a trail of your clothing leading to your love nest!

You and your Pisces Guy will have an easy time being together as long as you allow him to be himself. He'll never be perfect, but he's a kind, sweet partner and passionate lover. He needs you to keep him grounded, and you need him to send your spirit flying.

Libra

Your Pisces Guy is an enigma to most people, but you can figure him out in pretty short order. You talk a lot about the world of aesthetics, and you like the way his spiritual perspective brings more depth and meaning to your life.

Speaking of deep things, your Pisces Guy certainly knows how to touch you sexually in areas where no man has gone before. He can turn you from an intellectual, chirpy conversationalist into a moaning, groaning orgasm machine. His response to your own sexual adeptness is probably his inspiration.

Your household will be like a museum of sorts, filled with various works of art. Problems could arise when it comes to keeping it all clean and dust-free, though! Neither of you is much for rolling up your sleeves to run the vacuum or mop the floors.

You and your Pisces Guy have a marvelous time, but you need help dealing with real-world problems. You should always keep people in your lives that you both can trust to shepherd you through rough spots, especially when it comes to big decisions regarding finances or real estate. With this protection, you two can stick to the business of loving one another with mind, body, and spirit.

Scorpio

Even before you settled down with your Pisces Guy, you knew he would need you. By now, you're probably surprised at the wonderful things he brings to your life. You fit together perfectly and yearn to show one another just how deeply you are in love.

That's why your sex life is so incredible! You adore becoming one with another person, maybe even more than most people do. This doesn't make you a sex maniac: it means that you truly appreciate what it is to share on such an intimate level, and no one can partake in that with more enthusiasm than your Pisces Guy!

Living in the same space might be a bit of a challenge, though. While your Pisces Guy will enjoy the nest you build, he might not contribute to it as much as you believe he should. Don't volunteer to give your all, because when he doesn't give what you think he owes, you can begin to resent him.

There's no doubt you and your Pisces Guy will have to work on communication in your relationship. While you see him as a fun friend, he views you as his teacher. He'll have to work on being more of an equal partner.

Sagittarius

Your Pisces Guy represents a safe haven for you, a person who understands all the passions and desires you have. You serve the role of an authority figure to your Pisces Guy. He thinks you know so much more than he does, and he'll defer to you when it comes to getting facts and figures.

Sexually, there is plenty of passion between you! Your Pisces Guy will enjoy the way you come to him like a little puppy dog, and you'll adore his cuddly, gentle bedside manner.

Your home will probably suffer from your mutual habits that involve restlessness and a desire to explore. While you're travel-mad, he's a prolific daydreamer. Neither of you is much for tending to the details of grocery shopping or cleaning.

To keep your relationship healthy, you'll have to give up some of your wilder adventures and tend to his emotional needs. Pisces may be willing to follow you to the ends of the earth, but he isn't as hardy as you are. At home, at least, you can both count on the delights of that wonderful sex life of yours!

Capricorn

You and your Pisces Guy have a sweet little thing going, but you're going to have to work hard not to get frustrated with him. Pisces generally doesn't have his act together, but he believes he does. You'll have to save him now and then, but he'll do his best to make you happy.

Your Pisces Guy will adore the way you respond to his deep desire to please you. He'll also help you push the envelope just enough to get you out of your emotional shell.

If you look to your Pisces Guy to take care of your home or be the one who brings home the lion's share of income, you might be disappointed. Most Pisces Guys aren't interested in material rewards. He can paint and do landscaping, but you might want to call professionals for plumbing and electricity work.

Staying with your Pisces Guy will require a lot of concessions on your part, but if you let him, this warm and wonderful creature will shower you with appreciation. Pisces holds the keys to a gate that leads you to the world of spirit and eternal love. Join him there to reap the fruits of your patience and love. You deserve it.

Aquarius

You and your Pisces Guy might not seem to have lots in common, but you'll fool everybody when they see how much you love being together. Your relationship is a microcosm of the way each of you demonstrates heartfelt empathy for all humanity.

You'll discover, through making love with the deeply intuitive and spiritual Pisces Guy, that there's so much more to life than getting others to see your point. When you're having sex with him, you'll experience an emotional awakening you might not have thought possible!

Your home will be interesting to say the least. Between the two of you, there could be quite a collection of objects! While you'll favor items with clean lines and modern proclivities, your Pisces Guy will love antiques and *objects d'art* that evoke your and his spiritual life.

Keeping together will be easy, as long as you remember what you bring to one another's lives. He offers you a more spiritual viewpoint, while you give him the structure and direction he needs to discipline his thoughts. By bringing out the best in one another, you create a couple that's well worth the alterations and efforts.

Pisces

You and your Pisces Guy are not particularly attached to the material world. This won't stop you from building a viable, enjoyable life together, though! He'll love the way you stand quietly by and allow him to do his thing, and you'll appreciate how he believes in everything you do.

In the bedroom, you offer the ultimate in sensitivity and deep, true love through the orgasmic experience. He'll respond just the way you do to stimulation, with an experience of ecstasy that lets you know how much he loves you.

You must cherish him—and his household possessions—the way you wish to have him respect you and yours. Use your creative abilities to design a space that reflects a little bit of both of you. You'll enjoy quiet getaways, too, especially if you get to be near the water.

You and your Pisces Guy will have to work hard to count your money, pay the bills, and take care of business. If you put your two heads together, you can figure things out. If not, get expert help. All that really matters is you're there for each other—two fish swimming in an eternal circle of respect, affection, and true love.

YOUR PISCES GUY AND . . .

Your Pisces Guy will do his best to blend into your life, but reading here will give you some information about how he might interact with other significant people and things, so you can avoid unpleasant surprises.

Your Female Friends

Your Pisces Guy will embrace your female friends, calling many of them his own. This might disturb you at first, but there's no hanky-panky going on here! Your Pisces Guy is attracted to the feminine softness most women exude, and he appreciates their interest in the things he does with his imagination. You'll just have to share your friends with him. They'll love him, too.

Your Male Friends

Your Pisces Guy will tolerate your male friends, but tread very lightly on his delicate feelings. If he senses one of them can give you something he's not capable of giving, he'll be very hurt to see you spend a lot of time with them. Always try to include him and tell your male buddies how proud you are of your Pisces Guy.

His Female Friends

Your Pisces Guy attracts many female friends, but most of them truly have only platonic intentions. His softness and sensitivity invite them to use him as a confidante. They'll tell him all their problems and know he'll keep their secrets. Watch that he doesn't get overburdened, though. He tends to take others' issues on as his own, so help him create healthy boundaries.

His Male Friends

Your Pisces Guy won't likely be hanging out at the ball games or the poker table. He doesn't like rough locker room talk, though he'll tolerate it at times. If he has a group of artistic types or charitable workers he shares a common bond with, then he'll easily mesh with them and consider their meetings to be a safe and happy place.

Your Family

Your family will probably have as much trouble as you do pinning down exactly what your Pisces Guy is about, but just like you, they'll like him. There's that empathic quality he has that always allows him to relate to what people are going through. His sympathetic ear and wild imagination allow him to get along with everyone from Granny to your grandnephews.

His Family

Your Pisces Guy will probably be close to his family, but not always in the healthiest connection to them. He will do a lot of things for them, but he could also find himself being victimized by some more manipulative family members. They sense he'll do anything for their love, and take advantage of him. You can step in and protect him. He'll really appreciate that.

Your Pets

Your pets will probably sense your Pisces Guy's coming for a visit before you know he's there. His way of communicating in the world without words helps him connect to your pets, and he'll be sincerely enamored with them. Although he'll still let you do most of the care-taking, he'll be like that favorite uncle to them . . . the one everybody loves because he spoils them to death!

His Pets

Your Pisces Guy isn't one to keep a lot of animals around his house, but it's not because he doesn't like them. Pets can really tap in to his ethereal energies, and in some cases, wear him out. Other Pisces Guys will gain more energy from communicating with their pets, and thus keep a pack of dogs or a den of cats to keep them company and provide sweet entities to love.

His Potential for Success

While some Pisces Guys have an easy time taking care of their financial needs, even they aren't primarily motivated by money or worldly success. Your Pisces's heart is made to give more than it receives, at least in the material sense. He'd rather share his talents than amass a fortune, but if you tell him that by earning good money he's taking care of your family, he'll put more focus on income.

His Role as a Father

A Pisces father will be kind and understanding, sweet and unassuming, doting and not very daring. Children will love him, because he tells them everything always will turn out all right as long as they put the focus on love. You may need to step in on disciplinary matters, because Pisces just can't stand the sight of his child in time-out or getting grounded on the night of the big dance.

PISCES COMPATIBILITY	
Your Sign	**Compatibility Levels**
Aries	♈
Taurus	♉♉
Gemini	♊♊♊
Cancer	♋♋♋♋♋
Leo	♌♌
Virgo	♍♍♍♍♍
Libra	♎♎♎
Scorpio	♏♏♏♏
Sagittarius	♐♐♐♐
Capricorn	♑♑
Aquarius	♒
Pisces	♓♓♓

PISCES SHORT-TERM PROSPECTS	
Your Sign	**Short-Term Prospects**
Aries	♈♈
Taurus	♉♉♉
Gemini	♊♊♊
Cancer	♋♋♋♋♋
Leo	♌
Virgo	♍♍♍♍
Libra	♎♎
Scorpio	♏♏♏
Sagittarius	♐♐♐
Capricorn	♑
Aquarius	♒
Pisces	♓♓♓

PISCES LONG-TERM PROSPECTS	
Your Sign	**Long-Term Prospects**
Aries	♈♈
Taurus	♉
Gemini	♊♊♊♊
Cancer	♋♋♋♋♋
Leo	♌♌
Virgo	♍♍♍♍
Libra	♎♎
Scorpio	♏♏♏
Sagittarius	♐♐♐♐
Capricorn	♑♑
Aquarius	♒
Pisces	♓♓♓♓

ABOUT THE AUTHOR

Judi Vitale is an accomplished astrologer and writer. She currently does the research behind the horoscopes for *Marie Claire*, and has written astrology columns, articles, and reports for a variety of magazines and websites. These have included Seventeen.com, the UK's *prima* magazine, *AstroGirl* magazine, *Redbook* magazine, and Tarot .com. She is also a certified Consulting Astrologer of the NCGR Professional Astrologers' Alliance. She holds a Masters Degree in Public Administration from the University of Pittsburgh and is an alumna of Carnegie Mellon's College of Humanities and Social Sciences, where she studied history.

Judi began to study astrology when she was quite young—somewhere around the time they declared the dawning of the Age of Aquarius! She intensified her study of astrology during the 1980s, and began writing horoscopes for publication in 1998.

Having relocated to Pittsburgh after many years in New York City, Judi has come "home" to rejoin family and many friends. She maintains an active client practice, and continues to marvel at the magical way astrology helps us to understand ourselves and the significant others in our lives. Judi feels privileged to convey to others the knowledge that things always turn out the way they're supposed to, especially when there is unconditional, unending love.

Lovecasts is Judi's first book, but she intends to write many, many more. She was born under the sign of Cancer, and treasures her home life, especially cooking. She also enjoys living near her college-age son, a confirmed Libra, and with a fiercely clever Tibetan Terrier (a spunky Aries) called "Hairiette."

BEYOND HERE

Sure, this world is fascinating, but what's beyond is even more intriguing...

Want a place to share stories and experiences about all things strange and unusual? From UFOs and apparitions to dream interpretation, the Tarot, astrology, and more, the **BEYOND HERE** blog is the newest hot spot for paranormal activity!

Sign up for our newsletter at

www.adamsmedia.com/blog/paranormal

and download our free Haunted U.S. Hot Spots Map!